Charles Francis Routledge

The Church of St. Martin, Canterbury

An illustrated account of its history and fabric

Charles Francis Routledge

The Church of St. Martin, Canterbury
An illustrated account of its history and fabric

ISBN/EAN: 9783337260712

Printed in Europe, USA, Canada, Australia, Japan

Cover: Foto ©ninafisch / pixelio.de

More available books at **www.hansebooks.com**

THE CHURCH OF
ST. MARTIN
CANTERBURY

ST. MARTIN'S CHURCH (SOUTH SIDE).

THE CHURCH OF
ST. MARTIN
CANTERBURY

AN ILLUSTRATED ACCOUNT OF
ITS HISTORY AND FABRIC

BY THE

REV. C. F. ROUTLEDGE, M.A., F.S.A.

HON. CANON OF CANTERBURY

LONDON GEORGE BELL & SONS 1898

W. H. WHITE AND CO. LTD.
RIVERSIDE PRESS, EDINBURGH

PREFACE

THE associations connected with St. Martin's Church are manifold, and of universal interest. During recent explorations so much fresh matter has been brought to light that it has become almost necessary to re-write the structural description of the building, and to re-consider the date of its foundation. We have endeavoured to lay before our readers a plain summary of the discoveries that have been made, and to elucidate them, as far as possible, from the pages of history---for (in the words of a sound antiquary) "It is every day more true that people *want* history in guide-books. The tourist is a much better informed person than he used to be, and desires to be still more so."

CHARLES F. ROUTLEDGE.

CANTERBURY,
May 1898.

CONTENTS

PAGE

CHAPTER I.—Introduction   3
   Early Christianity in Britain   6

CHAPTER II.—History of the Church   14
   Roman Canterbury   15
   The Saxon Invasion   21
   The Mission of St. Augustine   24
   Baptism of Ethelbert   31
   Bishops of St. Martin's   34

CHAPTER III.—
   Description of the Church—Exterior   41
   Dedication   41
   Walls   45
   Buttresses   48
   Doorways   51
   Description—Interior   62
   Font   67
   West Wall of Nave   71
   Norman Piscina   74
   Chancel   76
   Chrismatory   83

APPENDIX A: List of Rectors   93
   B: Date of Church   94
   C: Eastern Apse, etc.   99

LIST OF ILLUSTRATIONS

	PAGE
St. Martin's Church (South Side). . .	*Frontispiece*
East End of Church (Cathedral in Distance) . .	2
West Front of Church (Exterior) . .	15
Plan of Roman Canterbury . .	17
Church in 1840 (Interior)	39
Plan of Church	42
S.-E. Angle of Nave (Foundations) .	49
Stukely's Engraving of Church . .	50
Foundations (under Panel) . . .	51
Mrs Parry's Sketch of S.-W. of Chancel	53
Wall above Adjunct	55
Saxon Doorway (Interior) . . .	57
Saxon Doorway (Exterior) . -	59
Font	65
West Wall of Nave . .	69
Roman Window .	72
Norman Piscina . .	75
Chancel (Photo) . .	77
Sedile	79
Queen Bertha's Tomb .	81
Chrismatory (Shut)	83
Chrismatory (Open) . .	85
St. Martin's (from Old Print)	91
Tracings of Apse—Appendix C	99

A

Photochrom Co. Ltd., Photo.

EAST END OF CHURCH (SHOWING CATHEDRAL IN THE DISTANCE).

ST. MARTIN'S CHURCH

CHAPTER I

INTRODUCTION

St. Martin's Church, both from its history and structure occupies a unique position. It is at once the cradle of purely *English* Christianity, and also a witness of that earlier Christianity which existed in Britain during the period of the Roman occupation. At the recent commemoration of the thirteen-hundredth anniversary of the "coming of St. Augustine," a solemn pilgrimage was made by the Archbishops and Bishops of the Anglican communion to this venerable church as being the *one* remaining building that could certainly be associated with St. Augustine's preaching; the *one* spot that without doubt felt his personal presence, whatever we may think of the more or less strong claims put forth on behalf of Ebb's Fleet, Richborough Castle, the ruins of St. Pancras, or the site of Canterbury Cathedral. In a prayer specially written for that occasion occurs the following passage: "We give Thee, O God, hearty thanks that by the preaching of Thy Blessed Servant Augustine, especially in this Holy House in which we are gathered together in Thy Name, Thou didst bring home the truth of the Gospel to our English forefathers, and didst call them out of darkness into Thy marvellous Light."

At the same time, those who were somewhat jealous of the claims of St. Augustine to be considered (as he often is by modern Roman Catholics) "the introducer of Christianity into this island," could point to the fact that, though the *ecclesia vetusta* of Glastonbury had disappeared, and its later abbey was in ruins, there was *here* some portion at least of an actual edifice stated by the Venerable Bede to have been "dedicated to the honour of St. Martin, and built of old, while the Romans were still occupying Britain,"—that is, at least 200 years before the advent of the Italian Mission.

Beyond this authentic passage, the proofs of its pre-Augustinian origin can be gathered only from the evidence of archæological research, upon which we shall enter hereafter: and we must to a great extent depend upon this same evidence for its subsequent history after 597 A.D., though it undoubtedly gave the title of "Bishops of St. Martin's" to some *chorepiscopi* before the Norman Conquest. The interesting detailed references to individual churches, usually gleaned from ancient Archidiaconal Visitation Registers, are wanting in this case, because the church is, and always has been, exempt from the jurisdiction of the Archdeacon of Canterbury, and we can derive little or no information from the archives at Lambeth, since the Archiepiscopal visitations were, as a rule, merely diocesan and not parochial.

The church is situated on a gently-sloping hill, about a thousand yards due east of the cathedral.

To one looking from the elevated terrace which bounds its churchyard, the panorama is exceedingly picturesque and beautiful. In the distance rises a range of low wooded hills that almost encircle Canterbury, and the conspicuous building of Hales' Place, now the Jesuits' College; while beneath is spread in a hollow the city itself, with its red-tiled roofs interspersed with patches of green, the library and twin towers of St. Augustine's Abbey, and above all the massive cathedral, with "Becket's Crown" in the foreground, and the central "Bell Harry" tower lifting out of the morning's mist its magnificent pinnacles and tracery.

The prospect to Dean Stanley's eye was "one of the most inspiriting that could be found in the world," because of its religious associations, and its reminder that great and lasting good could spring from the smallest beginning. But even in its physical aspect, it is one that, in England at least, can seldom be surpassed; and in olden times the view must have been even more grand and extensive than it is at present, as the church stood in almost solitary grandeur, a permanent brick and stone edifice, above the wooden buildings nestling among thickets of ash—fit emblem of the durability of Divine, as compared with the perishable nature of human, institutions.

It must even then have been somewhat of a marvel, on account of the rare mode of its construction, for at that early epoch churches were usually built of hewn oak, and the stone church of St. Ninian's at Whithern is specially mentioned by Bede as having been erected " in a manner unusual among the Britons."

The hill itself, on its northern and eastern sides, is honeycombed with springs, from which down to a late period the city was supplied with water. We can imagine it studded here and there with Roman villas, of which some remains in the shape of tesselated pavements were discovered two or three centuries ago—and crowned possibly by a small Roman encampment ; while the church, situated only a few yards off the road to Richborough, would frequently have been seen and admired by soldiers on their march from the sea coast to the great fortress of London, or to the southern stations at Lympne and Dover.

Imagination would picture to itself the reverence felt for so sacred and venerable a spot, yet the fact remains, that up to a recent date the present church was regarded simply as a memorial of the past, a monument erected on the site of the ancient edifice, and reproducing some of its characteristic materials.

Mr Matthew W. Bloxam, for instance, in his preliminary observations to the " Principles of Gothic Ecclesiastical Architecture," after giving a sketch of its history and ancient fame, declares that it was *rebuilt* in the twelfth or thirteenth century, though to all appearance with the materials of the original church. Even Dean Stanley, who cherished for it a fond and enthusiastic love, assures us that, old as the present church is, " it is of far later date than Bertha's Chapel " ; while so close an observer of archæological facts as the late Mr Thomas Wright sweeps away all question as to its traditional continuity by stating boldly that " not a trace of Christianity is found among the innumerable religious and sepulchral monuments of the Roman period in Britain ! "

It has been pertinently observed, that " these are conclusions too hastily arrived at ; and antiquaries should ever remember that their facts of to-day may receive fresh additions, illustrations, and corrections from the discoveries of to-morrow," — for since 1880 a series of explorations

carried out both above and below ground, and a minute investigation into the character of the existing masonry, have
made it more than probable that parts of the original structure
mentioned by Bede are still standing, and that the present
walls were not only consecrated by the preaching, and actually
touched by the hand, of St. Augustine, but may be traced
back to a considerably earlier period.

The church has survived its period of apparent disuse
after the Roman departure from Britain. It escaped the
destructiveness of the Jutes, and the devastation inflicted on
Canterbury by the Danish invaders, and has been preserved
to us (as we hope to show hereafter) a venerable and genuine
relic of Romano-British Christianity. It suffered, indeed,
after the Norman Conquest, both from centuries of neglect
and also from so-called restoration—becoming at one time
what Mr Ruskin would call "an interesting ruin," at another
time being plastered and modernised till its ancient features
were almost obliterated; but even when enemies were attack-
ing religion from without, and faith grew cold within, the
worship of Almighty God was carried on continuously under
the shadow of its sacred walls, and on its altar for more than
thirteen centuries has been offered the Sacrifice of the Holy
Eucharist.

History is silent as to its builder—silent as to the exact date
of its foundation. In the simple words of Fuller, "The Light
of the Word shone here, but we know not who kindled it."

The mere fact of the existence of such a church involves of
necessity the further question as to its immediate origin,
whether it be attributed to Roman Christians, or to British
converts working under the influence, if not the direct super-
intendence, of their conquerors. And in discussing this, we
must perforce touch lightly the fringe of that well-worn, yet
ever-fascinating, inquiry respecting the "earliest introduction of
Christianity into Britain"—difficult as it is in ancient traditions
and allusions to dissociate fact from fiction, genuine documents
from forgeries, history from legend, so eager were the so-called
writers of ecclesiastical history to advance their theories, even
at the expense of truth.

We may indeed derive some assistance from the fact which
we learn from secular historians, that in Apostolic times there
was frequent communication between Rome and Britain.

After the first conquest of Britain, Roman governors were sent in almost uninterrupted succession, and with them would come, of course, legions and cohorts, perhaps even some of the Prætorian soldiers in whose company the apostle St. Paul lived for a time during the reign of Nero. British chieftains were taken prisoners to Rome, and their sons left there as hostages. Some few Romans, too, such as Seneca, the brother of Gallio, held large possessions in the island. People and places connected with Britain are mentioned by the Roman poets Martial and Juvenal, and by the historian Tacitus. With such constant intercourse as there must have been, stories at least and reports of Christianity would have been brought over to the island as early as the first century, and there were probably individual Christians either among the numerous soldiers quartered here, or among returned captives. We may be doubtful whether at so early an epoch, save perhaps in a few exceptional cases, they formed themselves into regular societies or congregations, and it is not likely that they erected for themselves permanent places of worship. No such antiquity as this can be claimed even for the remains of the Roman church found amid the ruins of Silchester; and church building, as it is generally understood, did not begin at Rome before the fourth century, and it would have taken a few years to spread thence to Gaul, and from Gaul to Britain.

That Christianity did exist in Britain from early times, in a more or less settled form, is no longer a matter of dispute. In the words of Gildas, "Christ, the true Son, offered His rays (*i.e.* His precepts) to this island, benumbed with icy coldness, and lying far distant from the visible sun. I do not mean from the sun of the temporal firmament, but from the Sun of the highest arch of heaven, existing before all time." Relative to this fact there are a few statements of ancient writers given at dates which are precisely known, during the third century and subsequently: and these statements are familiar to all students, so that they need not be recapitulated at any length. Tertullian (in 208), Origen (in 239), Eusebius (about 320), allude in unmistakable terms to the existence of British Christianity, however rhetorical the passages may appear.

There is, too, the account of the martyrdom of *St. Alban*, recorded at length in the pages of Bede, which cannot be treated as an idle legend. It took place at Verulam during the persecution under Diocletian and Maximian, somewhere about 303. Although the record does not rest on contemporary evidence, the story was fully believed at Verulam itself as far back as 429 A.D. (*i.e.* within a hundred and twenty-six years of the traditional date) and is accepted by Constantius in the fifth, as well as by Gildas and Venantius Fortunatus in the sixth, century—while the difficulty of believing in the possibility of a persecution in Britain, which was then under the kindly and tolerant rule of Constantius, seems to us purely imaginary. It is hardly probable that Constantius would have been able to restrain the persecuting zeal of subordinates, in face of the superior authority of Maximian, who is said by Gibbon to have "entertained the most implacable aversion to the name and religion of the Christians." Dean Milman sees no reason for calling in question the historic reality of the event, and suggests that the probable fact of St. Alban being a Roman soldier may have been an additional reason for his not having received the "doubtful protection" of Constantius.

But after this period we come to even surer ground—and from the beginning of the fourth century we find a Christian church fully organised in Britain. At the Council of Arles (in 314) three British bishops were present, whose very names and dioceses are recorded—viz. Eborius of York, Restitutus of London, and Adelphius of Caerleon-on-Usk or Lincoln. British bishops took part in the Councils of Sardica (347) and Ariminium (359), and probably also in the great Council of Nicæa (325). We have also testimony to a regular organisation in the pages of St. Chrysostom, Jerome, Theodoret, etc., ranging from the end of the fourth to the beginning of the fifth century. The conversion of the Southern Picts by Ninian, Bishop of Whithern—the visits of Germanus, Bishop of Auxerre, and Lupus, Bishop of Troyes, to Verulam and elsewhere—the missions of Palladius and Patrick to Ireland—the pilgrimages of British Christians to the Holy Land—and even the fact of the Pelagian heresy being propagated by a Briton—all equally bear witness to the prevalence of Christianity in these early centuries, so that Gildas may not be drawing entirely on his imagination when he describes the Church as "spread over the nation, organised, endowed, having sacred edifices and altars, the three orders of the ministry and monastic institutions, embracing the people of all ranks and classes, and having its own version of the Bible, and its own ritual."

Now, in view of these facts, many writers have not unnaturally endeavoured to trace the introduction of Christianity to some great man, or to some special effort. It seemed so impossible that a complete organisation should have sprung up without a definite founder—and claims have been made on behalf of St. Peter, St. John, Simon Zelotes, and Aristobulus, though without even a shadow of probability to recommend them. Something, indeed, may be urged in favour of the pious belief that St. Paul made his way to this island between his first and second imprisonment. St. Clement of Rome says that he preached "to the extreme boundary of the West"; St. Chrysostom, that from Illyricum "he went to the very ends of the earth"; and Theodoret, that the Apostles, including St. Paul, "brought to all men the laws of the Gospel, and persuaded not only the Romans . . . but also the Britons, to receive the laws of the Crucified," while the theory has received the support of Soames, Bishop Burgess, Collier, and other ecclesiastical writers—even Bishop Lightfoot thinking it " not improbable that the western journey of St. Paul included a visit to Gaul," from which an extension of his journey to Britain would not of course be impossible. It is true, too, that (as with the closing years of St. Peter) there is an interval of time after St. Paul's first imprisonment (variously estimated as from four to eight years) which cannot be accounted for ; and that the mere fact of silence as to St. Paul having preached in this island need not be unduly pressed, because Britain was at that time an obscure and unimportant province at the extremity of the Roman empire. But the critical historian cannot accept what is, after all, a mere conjecture, unsupported by long tradition or any positive evidence—any more than he can lay stress upon what is only a curious coincidence, between the mention by Martial of Claudia, a British lady in Rome newly married to Pudens—and the salutation of "Claudia and Pudens" in St. Paul's Second Epistle to Timothy, written from Rome. The theory as to this identification, is based on a string of hypotheses, called by Dean Farrar "an elaborate rope of sand." Similar remarks would also apply to the legend that the father of Caractacus, King of the Silures, called Bran the Blessed, was converted to Christianity when captive at

Rome (A.D. 51-58) and introduced the Gospel into his native
country on his return, though there is a tradition to that effect
incorporated into the Welsh Triads, which are probably none
of them earlier than the fourteenth century. Tacitus (Ann.
xii. 35) only mention the "wife, daughter and brothers" of
Caractacus as having surrendered with him, and he would
scarcely have omitted the "father," if he had shared their
captivity.

There is, indeed, one story which we are very loath to
surrender—viz. the story that St. Joseph of Arimathea was
sent, with twelve companions, to Britain by the Apostle St.
Philip (about 63 A.D.) settled in the Isle of Avalon or Glastonbury, and founded there a monastery, striking his staff into the
earth, and making it burst, like Aaron's rod, into leaf, and
bloom with the blossom of the Holy Thorn. This legend,
indeed, is not actually recorded in writing before William of
Malmesbury in the twelfth century, but it may have rested on
earlier local tradition. We know that Glastonbury was a
Christian sanctuary before the Saxons conquered the district,
and Bishop Browne (of Bristol) reminds us that Domesday Book
speaks of the "twelve *hides* (the portions of land said to have
been granted to St. Joseph's companions) which never have been
taxed," and that at the Council of Basle in 1431 the English
Church claimed and received precedence as founded by St.
Joseph of Arimathea in Apostolic times. The tradition, too,
that the first British Christians erected at Glastonbury a church
made of twigs or wattlework (called afterwards the *Vetusta
Ecclesia*, and only destroyed by fire in 1184) has been illustrated, if not confirmed, by recent discoveries at Glastonbury
(among the ruins of British houses burned with fire) of baked
clay showing the impress of wattlework. There is no known
fact connected with the life of St. Joseph of Arimathea that
would negative the conclusion that he might have been sent to
Britain as a missionary.

Some difficulties would be solved if we could believe the
tale about Lucius, a British King, having requested Eleutherius,
Bishop of Rome from 171 to 185, to send someone to teach
his people Christianity. This legend is recorded by Bede,
partly confirmed by Nennius, and accepted by William of
Malmesbury. And the name of Lucius has been variously
associated with Winchester, Gloucester, Llandaff, St. Peter's

Cornhill, St. Martin's Church, St. Mary's Church in Dover Castle, and even the church on the site of Canterbury Cathedral. The story probably owed its origin to a note in *Catalogus Pontificum Romanorum*, but it does not occur in the earlier catalogue written about 353, and was added to it nearly two hundred years later, with the object apparently of connecting the primitive growth of Christianity in Britain with the See of Rome. Though this ancient story cannot be considered as historical, it is not altogether impossible that it had some foundation in an application from a British prince to receive instruction in Christianity about the end of the second century: and this would give point to the statement of Tertullian (in 208) that "the kingdom and name of Christ were venerated in districts of Britain not yet reached by the Romans."

There is much force in the conclusion arrived at by Bishop Browne, that, "with Gaul so close at hand, its people so near of kin, its government so identical with theirs, the Britons would learn Christianity from, and through, Gaul," to whose church ours should occupy the position of a younger sister. At the same time, this fact must be considered—viz. that the earliest bishops mentioned as having attended the Council of Arles are anterior in point of time to the dated bishops in a great majority of the dioceses of Gaul adjacent to this island, so that we should not too readily abandon the possible belief that there was an independent church in Britain, though we know not *when* or *by whom* it was founded.

It only remains in this chapter to mention a few of the traces of British Christianity as supplied by monumental or other evidence well attested. We may believe, with Bede, that over St. Alban's tomb at Verulam, "when the peace of the Christian times returned, a church was built of wonderful workmanship, and worthy of that martyr"; and three churches are spoken of at Caerleon, two of which were dedicated to Julius and Aaron, said to have been martyred in the Diocletian persecution; another at Bangor Iscoed, near Chester; besides one at Candida Casa or Whithern, and the Vetusta Ecclesia at Glastonbury, our own church of St. Martin, and the foundations of that lately discovered in Roman Silchester. This is a fair number, even if we pass over for the time any possible claims to Roman origin on the part of Brixworth, Lyminge, Reculver, and St. Mary's Church in Dover Castle, all of which are ascribed to the Saxon period by Mr J. T. Micklethwaite in his interesting paper read at Canterbury in 1896 before the meeting of the Royal Archæological Institute— though we need not allow that his reasoning is in all cases indisputable.

We possess, too, some sepulchral monuments and inscriptions (not at present very extensive, but probably greatly to be multiplied as fresh excavations and explorations are made) at St. Mary le Wigfred, Lincoln, Caerleon, and Barming, and the *Chi-Rho* monogram (which was first introduced as a Christian symbol by the Emperor Constantine at the beginning of the fourth century) on various rings, stones, and tesselated pavements, also crosses on pavements at Harpole and Harkstow, and various Christian formulas such as "Vivas in Deo," "In pace," etc.

The dogmatism and incredulity of antiquaries may well be illustrated in the case of Mr T. Wright ("The Celt, the Roman, and the Saxon"). He disbelieves in all traces of Christianity said to be found among monuments of the Roman period; and his scepticism is thorough and comprehensive—more extreme in our opinion than the credulity which he denounces. He allows, indeed, the possibility of there having been some individuals among recruits and merchants and settlers who had embraced the truths of the Gospel, but with a qualification. He thinks the early allusions made by Tertullian, Origen, Jerome, and others are "little better than flourishes of rhetoric." The list of British bishops at the Council of Arles seems to him "extremely suspicious, much like the invention of a later period." He disbelieves the whole account of the Diocletian persecution having extended to Britain, even partially or locally. He doubts the authenticity of the work attributed to Gildas, though his objections have been met and set at rest, for most people, by such competent authorities as Dr Guest and others. But, as an instance of what I cannot but designate as far-fetched scepticism, we may note his explanation of the Christian monogram found on the pavement of a Roman villa at Frampton. He does not question its genuineness, but explains it by surmising that the beautiful villa had probably belonged to some wealthy proprietor, who possessed a taste for literature and philosophy, and with a tolerant spirit, which led him to surround himself with the memorials of all systems, had adopted, among the rest, that which he might learn from some of the imperial coins to be the emblem of Christ—Jesus Christ standing, in his eyes, on the same footing as Pythagoras or Socrates.

Surely we have here a warning against the dogmatism which is often indulged in by archæological experts, and it may be extended from monuments and remains to legends and traditions, which are often of great weight, even when they cannot be historically proved. It is not unnatural that many people should have become impatient and wearied of such purely negative criticism.

CHAPTER II

HISTORY OF THE CHURCH

BEFORE coming to the more immediate history of St. Martin's Church, we must say a few words about the Roman occupation of Canterbury, and the events preceding the landing of St. Augustine.

The city is mentioned in the second "iter" of Antonine's Itinerary, under its ancient name of Durovernum or Duroverno, a word supposed to be compounded of *dour*, "water," and *vern*, which has been variously interpreted to mean "temple," "marshes," or "alders."

Its position is described as fifty-two miles distant from London, fourteen from Dover, sixteen from Lympne, and twelve from Richborough; and the road from London to each of these last-named places divided itself at this point into three, crossing the ford of the River Stour, so that it would be a natural station for troops on the march.

The Egyptian geographer, Ptolemy, apparently writing about the middle of the second century, gives Durvĕnum as one of the three cities of the Cantii; while in the fragmentary map known as the *Tabula Peutingerii* (called so from Conrad Peutinger, in whose library it was found, and supposed to have been compiled about the time of the Emperor Theodosius the younger) it is put down as "Buroaverus," evidently a corruption of copyists, with the conventional mark usually attached to a city or fortress of considerable size.

Horsley, in his *Britannia Romana*, suggests that Canterbury was the fortress taken by the seventh legion after Julius Cæsar's second landing; but this is purely conjectural, and founded on the mistaken belief that Cæsar landed at Richborough. Even though the fact is not directly mentioned in the "Notitia Imperii" (enumerating the garrisons of the Empire), it is far from impossible that at some period or other

14

during the first four centuries there were some Roman soldiers quartered for a considerable time at Canterbury. If not wholly or partially surrounded by walls (which is more than probable), the city was at any rate defended by earthworks, and we have evidences of a fortified position held by the Romans immediately above the Whitehall marshes, north-

WEST FRONT OF ST. MARTIN'S CHURCH. (From an Old Print.)

west of the city; and of a stronghold or fort of masonry on the so-called Scotland Hills overlooking the Reed Pond.

Whether much stress be laid on this or not, one fact is absolutely certain, that the extensive Roman foundations discovered by Mr Pilbrow while constructing the deep-drainage system of the city in 1868, the number of Roman tesselated pavements, coins, and other relics found at various periods, and the traces of Roman cemeteries, abundantly prove that Durovernum developed at length into a large and populous place.

Among various discoveries may be enumerated Samian ware, coffins, conduit pipes, rings, bottles, urns, Upchurch pottery, spoons, arrowheads, and skeletons, as well as indications of a large iron foundry; and a long list of gold ornaments includes portions of châtelaines, fibulæ, studs, purses, combs ; and (what is especially germane to this history) a purple enamelled Roman brooch of circular shape, and a looped Roman intaglio, found near St. Martin's Church. All these appear to show that the Roman occupation of Canterbury was at once complete and continuous.

Of Roman secular buildings above ground there are indeed no remains, and the ancient city must be traced some eight feet below the present level. But in St. Margaret's and in Sun Street there are undoubted evidences of Roman walls. It is not impossible that, when first occupied, the town of Durovernum was very small, consisting of a citadel surrounded by earth mounds, and that it gradually extended itself afterwards beyond its original limits.

The elegance of some of the enamelled brooches and rings, together with other discoveries, point to a considerable degree of luxury and civilisation. One writer fancied that he detected the remains of raised seats for spectators at a circus or amphitheatre in the so-called Martyr's Field, near the London, Chatham, and Dover Railway Station.

The exact dimensions and extent of the city are open to some doubt. Mr T. Godfrey Faussett fixed the site of the four gates as follows :—(1) *Worth Gate*, at the end of Castle Street ; (2) *Riding Gate*, on the old road to Dover ; (3) *North Gate*, near the present south-west tower of the Cathedral ; and (4) a gate *at the Ford*, in Beer Cart Lane. Tracing the walls that lie between them, he concluded that the shape of the Roman town was an irregular oval, different from the usual square or rectangle, but accounted for by the low swampy ground that surrounded it, and not unlike the shape of Verulam and Anderida. The city's length, according to his plan, must have been nearly exactly double its breadth—namely 800 yards by 400.

For actual existing buildings that may possibly have been connected with the Roman occupation, we must have recourse to the *churches*, which supply us with traces of early Christianity more rich and numerous than that of any other town in England. These are to be found in St. Martin's, St. Pancras, and a church on the site of the present Cathedral. Detailed investigation of them would bring us to some controversial points, for

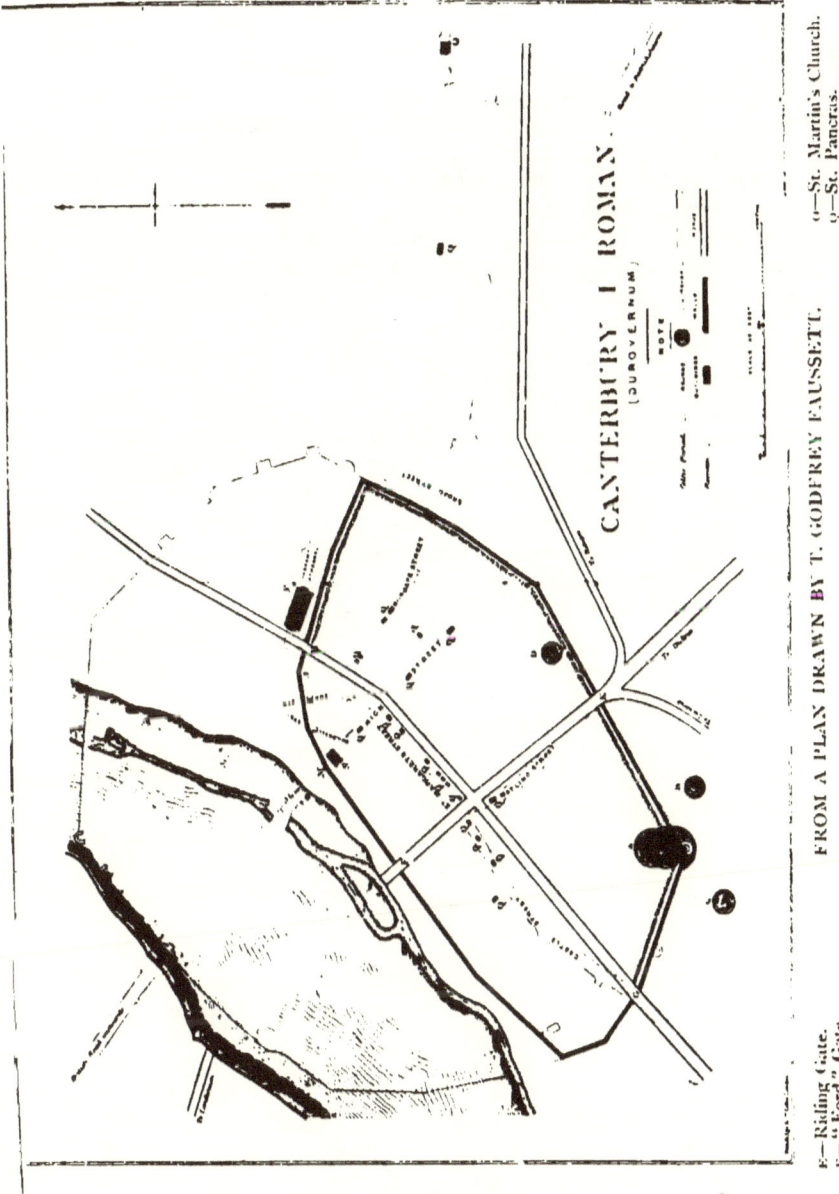

CANTERBURY I ROMAN
(DUROVERNUM)

FROM A PLAN DRAWN BY T. GODFREY FAUSSETT.

E.— Riding Gate.
F.— "Ford" Gate.
G.— Worth Gate.
H.— North Gate.

O.—St. Martin's Church.
Q.—St. Pancras.
P.—Site of First Cathedral.

17   B

the discussion of which one must be thoroughly conversant with all the recent discoveries and explorations that have been made.   But we may, at anyrate, state the *documentary* evidence.

With regard to *St. Martin's* Church, we have already quoted the statement made by the Venerable Bede.

The same historian also informs us that Augustine, "when the Episcopal See was granted to him in the royal city, recovered therein, supported by the king's assistance, a church which, he was informed, had been built by the ancient work of Roman believers ; and consecrated it in the name of our Holy Saviour, God and Lord, Jesus Christ."

He does not mention *St. Pancras*, but we are indebted for an account of it (evidently based on older traditions) to Thorn, a Benedictine monk of St. Augustine's, in the fourteenth century.   "There was not far from the city towards the east, as it were midway between the Church of St. Martin and the walls of the city, a temple or idol-house, where King Ethelbert, according to the rites of his tribe, was wont to pray, and with his nobles to sacrifice to his demons, and not to God—which temple Augustine purged from the pollutions and filth of the Gentiles ; and having broken the image which was in it, changed it into a church, and dedicated it in the name of the martyr St. Pancras ; and this was the first church dedicated by St. Augustine."   St. Pancras, a Roman boy of noble family, was martyred under Diocletian at the age of fourteen, and was regarded as the patron saint of children.   Dean Stanley reminds us that the monastery of St. Andrew on the Cœlian Hill, from which St. Augustine came, was built on the very property which had belonged to the family of St. Pancras, so that the name would have been quite familiar to the Roman missionary.

Now, these are the written traditions with regard to the early churches of Canterbury.   How far, then, are they confirmed by actual discoveries?   A great deal of light has been thrown upon the point within the last few years.   In the course of explorations conducted in the Cathedral crypt by Canon Scott Robertson, Dr Sheppard, and myself, there was found at the base of the western wall some masonry of Kentish ragstone covered by a smooth facing of hard plaster, manifestly older than the columns of Prior Ernulf's vaulting shafts, and than Lanfranc's masonry in the upper portion of the wall. We may, therefore, consider it as more than probable that a portion of this wall (which was laid bare to the length of twenty-seven feet) formed part of the original building granted to St. Augustine by King Ethelbert.

The ruins of St. Pancras have also been carefully and minutely investigated, and traces have been found there of both an undoubtedly Roman, and a somewhat later, build-ing. Though Mr J. T. Micklethwaite has satisfied himself that the present foundations can only be assigned to an Early Saxon period, asserting, indeed, that "we have evidence that it was used by St. Augustine himself," his arguments can not yet be accepted as conclusive, and much may be said on the other side.

We may observe an apparent difference in the shapes of these three churches. Of *St. Martin's* we shall speak at length hereafter, but we may note that, besides the different width of the nave and chancel, there is no sign of an apse at the west end, while indications of an eastern apse are more or less conjectural. In the plan of the original *Cathedral*, conjecturally drawn by Professor Willis from Edmer's description, and which he supposes was the old Christian church preserved by St. Augustine, the building was a plain parallelogram, with apses at both the east and west ends. The choir was extended into the nave, enclosed by a high breast-wall, and about the middle of the church (on the north and south) were two towers, the tower on the south side con-taining an altar, and also serving as a porch of entrance. This church was built, according to Edmer, "Romanorum opere," and in imitation of the Church of St. Peter, chief of the apostles, meaning the Vatican Basilica.

In *St. Pancras* there is a tower, or square porch, at the west end, and two transepts of the same size branching off from the centre of the nave, while the foundations of the chancel walls start farther in than those of the nave wall; and, at the distance of twelve or thirteen feet from the point of junction, can be detected the commencement of an apse. In this church we have discovered no doorways, except the one at the west end through the tower, and the possible indications of one leading into the southern transept, where we may yet see remains of an interesting altar (size, 4 ft. 4 by

2 ft. 2), which, if not the identical one that St. Augustine erected on the site occupied by the idol of Ethelbert, is at anyrate a very ancient memorial of it.

It is worthy of remark that these three churches are situated in almost a direct line from east to west, and were all outside the Roman walls, and apart from the Roman cemeteries. The orientation of all of them is nearly perfect.

In treating of the time between the departure of the Romans in 410 and the mission of St. Augustine in 597, we must remember that *history* is almost silent ; only a meagre outline of facts is given us, and these often of a very contradictory character. We must endeavour, however, to give a brief sketch of this intervening period as far as it concerns the south-eastern portion of our island, and of necessity, therefore, includes the fortunes of Canterbury. To account for the comparatively easy conquest of Britain in the middle of the fifth century, we are bidden to remember that the Roman rule, which had at first been of a civilising character, and had fostered commerce and the various arts, had in its latter period degenerated into corruption. Town and country alike were crushed by heavy taxation, aggravated by the arbitrary and ruinous oppression of the tax-gatherers. The population, too, had gradually declined as the estates of landed proprietors grew larger. Moreover, the Roman government had disarmed and enervated the people, and, by crushing all local independence, had crushed all local vigour, so that men forgot how to fight for their country, and constant foreign invasions found them without hope or energy for resistance.

Bishop Stubbs (in his " Constitutional History ") remarks on the great contrast between the effects of the Roman occupation in Gaul and Britain. Gaul had so assimilated the cultivation of its masters, that it became more Roman than Italy itself, possessing more flourishing cities and a more active and enlightened church, as well as a Latin language and literature ; while Britain, though equally under Roman dominion, had never become Roman. When the legions were removed, any union that may have existed between the two populations absolutely ceased. The Britons forgot the Latin tongue ; they had become unaccustomed to the arts of war, and had never learnt the arts of peace, while their clergy lost all sympathy with the growth of religious thought. They could not utilise the public works, or defend the cities of their masters, so that the country became easy to be conquered just in proportion as it was Romanised.

After a continuance of internal dissensions, described by Gildas in high-flown and rhetorical language, the native chiefs were once more troubled by piratical attacks, and by their Irish enemies. It was impossible to resist this combination by the forces of the province itself, and so, imitating that fatal policy of matching barbarian against barbarian, which led to the fall of the Roman Empire, the Britons summoned to their aid a band of English or Jutish warriors, to whom they promised food, clothing, pay, and grants of land. And this application for help was not unnatural, as there was probably in many of the towns a leaven of Teutonic settlers, especially along the "Saxon shore," who had maintained a steady intercourse with their kinsmen that remained behind, and some of whom may have been German war-veterans, pensioned off by successive Roman emperors.

The statement by Mr Green that the " History of England begins in 449 with the landing of Hengist and Horsa in the Isle of Thanet" is principally applicable to the *Kingdom of Kent*, for the Jutes had been preceded by Angles in the north, who seem to have been for some time in more or less undisputed possession of the country between the mouth of the Humber and the wall of Antoninus ; and the eastern shores of the island were to a great extent colonised by kindred tribes.

The leaders in this expedition naturally sent for reinforcements after their first successes, and it is probable that their followers were at the beginning contented with a settlement in the Isle of Thanet, where they would be secure against any possible treachery from the Britons, and would be near the sea, whence their compatriots would bring them aid if necessary— yet they gradually advanced, and their subsequent exploits culminated in the victory of Aylesford, six years after their landing, and the alleged death of the warrior Horsa.

This victory, it is said, was followed in Kent by a dreadful and unsparing massacre. The Jutes, merciless by habit, were provoked by the sullen and treacherous attitude of their victims, and destroyed all the towns which they captured. Some of the wealthier landowners of Kent fled in panic over the sea, but many of the poorer folk took refuge in forests, or escaped to Wales and Cornwall. Famine and pestilence devoured some, others were ruthlessly slaughtered. There was no means of escape, even by seeking shelter within the walls of their churches, since the rage of the English burnt fiercest against the clergy. The priests were slain at the altar, the churches burnt, and the peasants rushed from the flames, only to be cut down by the sword.

The above is the generally accepted theory, but probably in many respects it is an exaggerated account, such as is common in the traditions of conquered nations, and should be accepted with very great hesitation.

A few years after the victory of Aylesford, Richborough, Lympne, and Dover fell permanently into the hands of the invaders.

The Jutes, with whom Kent is more immediately concerned, were the northernmost of the three tribes of the Germanic family. They lived in the marshy forests and along the shores of the extreme peninsula of Denmark, which retains the name of Jutland to the present day. We know little of their early history, but it is probable that the Jutes, the Angles, and the Saxons, although speaking the same language, worshipping the same gods, and using the same laws, had no national or political unity—and the separate expeditions, resulting in the final conquest of Britain, were unconnected with one another, though almost continuous in point of time. It is certain that the invaders to a large extent declined to amalgamate with the people whom they had conquered; nor would they consent to tolerate their existence side by side. A few may have lingered on in servitude round the homesteads of their conquerors, but a large portion of the survivors (as we have said) took refuge in Western Britain.

As to their *religion*, we know that England for nearly a century and a half was almost entirely a heathen country, represented on a map as a black patch between the Christians of Gaul and the Christian Celts of our island. While the Goths, Vandals, Burgundians, and Franks in other parts of the Roman empire soon became Christians, the English went on worshipping their false gods, such as Woden, Thor, and others, who gave their names to river, homestead, and boundary alike, and even to the days of the week.

And yet their mythology was not so degraded but that it presented in fragments the outlines of Christianity. This was recognised afterwards by Pope Gregory's wise counsel to Augustine not to interfere needlessly with the religious faith of his pagan converts, but allow them to worship the old objects under new names; not to destroy the old temples, but to consecrate them as Christian churches, the reason being that "for hard and rough minds it is impossible to cut away abruptly all old customs, because he who wishes to reach the highest place must ascend by steps and not by jumps." Kemble (in his "Saxons in England") gives an insight into the character of their religion, and accounts for the ultimately rapid spread of Christianity among them by this process of adaptation, and also because the moral demands of the new faith did not seem to the Saxons more onerous than those to which they were previously accustomed. Bede not unnaturally reproaches the Britons for refusing or failing to convert their enemies to the true faith, whereas it had been the habit elsewhere for the Christian priesthood to act as mediators between barbarian invaders and the conquered.

Canterbury seems to have been at once abandoned by the vanquished, because it would have been utterly untenable owing to its position on the main road between the sea-fortresses of Kent and the rest of the kingdom : and it was probably at first unoccupied by the Jutes, so that it remained for many long years uninhabited and desolate. We know that the very name of Durovernum had become forgotten, while the fortresses of the coast still retained their former names without any radical change. This opinion is confirmed by the fact that, while numerous Saxon cemeteries have been found in East Kent—such as at Ash, Kingston, Sarre, etc.—none whatever have been discovered in the district immediately round Canterbury, though the soil has been thoroughly and completely turned over for the purposes of road and drain making, as well as for pits of gravel, sand, and chalk. More-over, not a single street of our city is on the site of a Roman street, with the partial exception of Watling Street and Beer Cart Lane.

Probably in the early days of the Jutish conquerors

Richborough would have been their headquarters, as being conveniently near the coast; and it was not till they had pretty well settled themselves in the country that they fixed on a new capital, to which they gave the name of *Cantwarabyrig*, "the city of the men of Kent."

The curtain of Christian history is not again lifted over England till the year 597, when, according to the "Anglo-Saxon Chronicle," "Gregory the Pope sent into Britain very many monks, who gospelled God's Word to the English folk." And, connected closely as the mission was with St. Martin's Church, we must enter into it with some detail, though it is an oft-told story, and is familiar even to those who have never visited Canterbury, and know little else of ecclesiastical history.

Gregory had been appointed at an early age "Prætor of the City" by the Emperor Justin II., and had afterwards been sent by Benedict I. and Pelagius II. to Constantinople, where he resided for many years as the representative of the Bishop of Rome. He returned to Rome in 585, and it was near this date that the event occurred which we are now about to narrate. He was at that time about forty-five years old, a monk in the great monastery of St. Andrew on the Cœlian Hill, which he had himself founded; and we may believe that he was remarkable, then as afterwards, for his comprehensive policy, his grasp of great issues, and his minute and careful attention to details in secular as well as religious matters. The vast slave trade prevalent in Europe was to him a special cause of sorrow; and for the purpose of trying to check the evil, to redeem the captives, or to mitigate their sufferings, he was wont to resort to the market-place in Rome whenever a new cargo of slaves arrived from distant countries.

One day, on his visit to the Forum of Trajan, he observed some (traditionally, *three*) boys with fair complexions, comely faces, and bright flowing hair, exposed for sale. When he saw them, he asked from what region or country they had been brought, and on being told "from the island of Britain, whose inhabitants were of similar appearance," inquired whether these islanders were Christians, or still involved in pagan errors. The answer was, "They are pagans." Then he heaved deep sighs from the bottom of his heart and said : "Alas! that men of such bright countenance should be subject to the author of darkness, and that such grace of outward form should hide minds void of grace within." Being told further, in answer to his question, that they were called *Angles*, " Rightly so called," said he, " for they have the faces of *Angels*, and are meet to be fellow-heirs with the angels in heaven. But what is the name of the province from which they were brought?" " *Deira* " (the land between the Tees and the Humber), said the merchant. " Right again," was the reply, " from wrath (*de ira*) shall they be rescued, and called to the mercy of Christ." Lastly, on hearing that the king of that province was named Ælla, he exclaimed : " Alleluia ! the praise of God the Creator shall be sung in those parts."

Gregory went from the Forum to the Pope (probably Pelagius), and asked him to send to the English nation some minister of the word, by whom the island might be converted to Christ, saying that he himself was prepared to undertake this work with the assistance of the Lord. But though the Pope gave his consent, so great was the love of the Roman people for him, that he was obliged to start from the monastery in the strictest secrecy, accompanied by a few of his comrades. When his departure became known, the people were much excited, and, dividing themselves into three companies, assailed the Pope as he went to church, crying with a *terrible voice* " What hast thou done? Thou hast offended St. Peter, thou hast destroyed Rome, since thou hast sent Gregory away." The Pope, greatly alarmed, despatched messengers with all possible speed to recall Gregory to Rome. He had already advanced three days along the great northern road when the messengers arrived, and led him back to the city.

Gregory afterwards become abbot of the monastery, and, much against his will, was elected Pope on the death of Pelagius, and consecrated on September 3, 590.

But he never forgot his project for the conversion of England, and in 595 wrote to Candidus, a priest in Gaul, directing him to use part of the Papal patrimony to purchase English youths of the age of seventeen or eighteen years, to be educated in monasteries, no doubt with the intention of sending them afterwards as missionaries to their countrymen.

It was not, however, till the following year that he was able to fulfil the desire of his heart, when he selected as the head of a mission to England Augustine, Prior of St. Andrew's Monastery, and charged him with letters to Vigilius, Bishop of Arles, to the Kings Theodoric and Theodebert, and to their grandmother, Queen Brunehaut or Brunichild. In the course of their journey, however, this missionary band was so terrified by the rumours they heard that they became faint-hearted on the road, and despatched Augustine to Rome to beg that they might be recalled. But Gregory would have no withdrawal, and sent him back again with letters of encouragement to his colleagues. So they went on, crossed the sea from Boulogne, and, either in the autumn of 596 or the early spring of 597, landed in England, somewhere in the Isle of Thanet.

The King of Kent at this time was *Ethelbert*, who was the most powerful King in England (reckoned by some as the third Bretwalda), and had established his supremacy over the Saxons of Middlesex and Essex, as well as over the English of East Anglia as far north as the Wash : and had driven back the West Saxons when, after an interval of civil feuds, they began again their advance along the Thames, and marched upon London. Ethelbert began to reign in 561. He was believed to be great-grandson of Eric, son of Hengist, a "son of the ash-tree." He had previously, when quite young, been engaged in an encounter with Ceawlin, King of Wessex, and been defeated at Wimbledon. But Ceawlin himself was worsted in 591 by his nephew Cedric at Woodnesbury, in Wiltshire ; and Ethelbert had now asserted his supremacy.

Unlike most English kings then, and for a long time afterwards, he had married a foreign wife, Bereta, or *Bertha*, daughter of Charibert, one of the kings of the Franks in Gaul, reigning in Paris. Bertha was a Christian, and, as Ethelbert was a heathen, it had been expressly stipulated, either by her father, or by her uncle and guardian Chilperic, King of Soissons, that she should enjoy the free exercise of her religion, and keep her faith inviolate.

Bertha is one of the most interesting and romantic characters in English history—our first Christian Queen—possessing apparently much the same influence over Ethelbert as Clotilda had done over Bertha's great ancestor, Clovis, and (though not able to convert him yet) without doubt disposing him

favourably towards the new religion. It is variously conjectured that she was born about 555 or 561. We do not
know much of her early life, but St. Gregory of Tours, in his
contemporary pages, informs us that King Charibert took to
wife, Ingoberga, by whom he had a daughter, who afterwards
"married a husband in Kent." Charibert was not a man of
good character, and being annoyed with his wife Ingoberga,
he forsook her, and married Merofledis, the daughter of a
certain poor woolmaker in the queen's service. The unfor-
tunate queen was thereupon obliged to fly, and, taking up her
abode at Tours, devoted herself to a life of religious seclusion,
bringing up her daughter Bertha under the direction of Bishop
Gregory, and preparing her thus for the part she afterwards
filled in the conversion of England. We may mention here
that King Charibert, after the death of Merofledis, proceeded
to marry her sister, for which outrage he was solemnly
excommunicated by St. Germanus : and, refusing to leave
her, "perished, stricken by the just judgment of God."
Ingoberga died at the age of seventy, in the year 589.

Bertha was accompanied to England by her chaplain,
Liudhard, who was sent with her to preserve her faith. Of
Liudhard we know very little that is certain. His name is
variously spelt Leotard, Liudhard, or even Liupard. By some
he was supposed to be Bishop of Senlis, but his name does not
occur in the list of bishops of that see, though it is inserted
with a mark of interrogation in Gow's *Series Episcoporum*.
By others he has been entitled Bishop of Soissons, though
without any documentary authority. We may probably accept
the notion that he was one of the "wandering bishops" who
were very numerous at a later period in Gaul. Gocelin calls
him the "faithful guardian of the queen." It seems strange
that he, who could speak a language akin to that of the
English, did not convert some of them previously to the
coming of Augustine, who only spoke Latin, and was obliged
to converse with them at first through the medium of an
interpreter.

However that may be, he was undoubtedly the "harbinger"
of Augustine, and had probably endeavoured to stir up his
brother prelates of Gaul on behalf of the English, since Pope
Gregory, writing at this time to Theodoric and Theodebert,
severely condemns the supineness of the Gallic Church, in

neglecting to provide for the religious wants of their neigh-
bours, whose "earnest longing for the grace of life had
reached his ears."

We may mention here that a coin was found some years
ago in the churchyard of St. Martin's, with the inscription,
"Lyupardus Eps"—and the Rev. Daniel Haigh (in his notes
on the Runic monuments of Kent) says that he has no doubt
that this coin belongs to Liudhard, who is called Liphardus in
Florus' addition to Bede's *Martyro-logia*.

Queen Bertha and her chaplain used to worship in the little
church of St. Martin, going there daily from Ethelbert's palace,
near the site of the present cathedral, through the postern gate
of the precincts opposite St. Augustine's gateway. To this circumstance, though by a somewhat fanciful etymology, is
attributed its name of *Queningate*. Owing to long disuse, it is
probable that the church had fallen into a state of partial decay,
but it was again restored and made suitable for Christian
worship—though the Queen, with her chaplain and attendant
maidens, may only have used a portion of the ancient building.

But we must now return to Augustine. "On the east of
Kent," says Bede, "is the large Isle of Thanet, containing,
according to the English way of reckoning, six hundred
families, divided from the mainland by the river Wantsum,"
which at that time was a channel nearly a mile in width,
running from Richborough to Reculver, though it has since
become a narrow ditch. Here was a small place called
Ebbsfleet, still the name of a farmhouse, rising out of Minster
Marsh, but, owing to the retreat of the sea, now situated among
green fields. There is little to catch the eye in Ebbsfleet itself,
which is a mere spit of higher ground, distinguished by its
clump of trees, but must then have been a headland, running
out into the sea. "Taken as a whole," says Mr Green, "the
scene has a wild beauty of its own. To the right, the white
curve of Ramsgate Cliffs looks down on the crescent of Peg-
well Bay. Far away to the left, across grey marshlands, where
smoke-wreaths mark the sites of Richborough and Sandwich,
rises the dim cliff-line of Deal." It is unnecessary to enter
into the controversy whether Augustine first set foot on English
ground here or at Stonar, or beneath the walls of the Roman
fortress of Richborough, as apparently stated by Thorn.
The whole question is fully discussed in an appendix to the

"Mission of St. Augustine," carefully compiled by Canon Mason.

The missionaries had no sooner landed than one or two of their body proceeded to Canterbury, where they duly acquainted King Ethelbert with the fact and object of their arrival. The king gave the messengers a favourable hearing, but bade them remain where they were, saying that he himself would visit them—making, however, this curious stipulation, that they should not hold their first interview under a roof, lest they should practise on him spells and incantations—"though they came," adds Bede, "furnished with Divine and not with magic power."

After some days, the king came to the island, where the interview took place, possibly under a large oak tree close to Cottington Farm, where a Sandbach Cross has been erected by the late Earl Granville as a memorial of the event and it was at this place that the commemoration of the "Coming of St. Augustine" was held in 1897, by the bishops of both the Anglican and Roman communions. Other traditions name the centre of the island, or the walls of Richborough but, wherever it was, the missionaries, on hearing of the king's arrival with his attendant thanes, came to meet him, chanting litanies, with a tall silver cross before them, and a figure of the Saviour painted on an upright board. Besides Augustine himself, who was of great stature, head and shoulders taller than anyone else, were Laurence, afterwards Archbishop of Canterbury, Peter, who became first Abbot of St. Augustine, and nearly forty others.

When the procession stopped, and the chant ceased, Ethelbert courteously bade the missionaries be seated. Then Augustine, through the medium of a Frankish interpreter, having preached to the king the Words of Life and the mercies of the Saviour, was answered by the king in the well-known passage :—"Fair indeed are your words and promises, but as they are new to us and of uncertain import, I cannot assent to them so far as to forsake that which I have so long held in common with the whole English nation. But because you have come as strangers from afar into my kingdom, and are desirous to impart to us those things which you believe to be true and most beneficial, we will not do you any harm, but rather receive

you in kindly hospitality, and take care to supply you
with necessary sustenance.   Nor do we forbid you to
preach, and win over as many as you can to the faith of
your religion."

The king was as good as his word. Before his return
to Canterbury, he gave orders that a suitable abode should
be prepared for the missionaries near the "Stable Gate,"
which stood not far from the present church of St. Alphege.

From the Isle of Thanet, Augustine and his companions
crossed the ferry to Richborough. Thence they proceeded
for about twelve miles almost due west to Canterbury,
passing by Ash and Wingham, and then between the
villages of Wickham and Ickham, till they came to St.
Martin's Hill. There they would catch sight of the little
church of St. Martin, which (as they well knew) had been
consecrated afresh to the worship of Jesus Christ, and of
the city below with its wooden houses dotted about among
the ash-groves.   As soon as they beheld the city, they
walked in procession down the hill, bearing aloft the silver
cross and the painted board—and as they passed St. Martin's
Church, the choristers, whom Augustine had brought from
Gregory's school on the Cælian Hill, chanted one of Gregory's
own litanies, "We beseech Thee, O Lord, in all Thy mercy,
let Thy wrath and anger be turned away from this city
and from Thy holy house, for we have sinned.
Alleluia!"

We can well imagine that the heathen inhabitants of
Canterbury must have been struck with astonishment at the
unwonted sight, as well as at the swarthy complexions and
strange dress of the Roman missionaries.   And we may
believe that Queen Bertha came forth to meet the band with
a feeling of intense joy. Whether Bishop Liudhard was still
alive or not, we have no evidence to determine.

Bede tells us that they began at once to imitate the
course of life practised in the primitive church, with frequent
prayer, watching, and fasting, preaching the word of life
to as many as they could, receiving only necessary food
from those whom they taught, living themselves conformably
to their teaching, being always prepared to suffer, even to
die, for the truth which they preached. In St. Martin's
Church they met, sang, prayed, celebrated mass, preached, and

baptised. And soon the firstfruits of their mission began to appear in the conversion and baptism of Ethelbert.

Ethelbert was baptised, according to an early tradition, on the Feast of Pentecost (June 2nd) in the year 597—but where? Of one thing there can be little doubt, that we should certainly expect him to have been baptised in St. Martin's Church. It was here that his queen had worshipped for so many years. It was here that Augustine is distinctly stated by Bede to have baptised—and so it was here (we may conclude with little hesitation) that the baptism of Ethelbert took place—even though we can find no direct statement to that effect earlier than that of John Bromton, writing at the end of the twelfth century, who says that "*there* (*i.e.* in St. Martin's) the king was baptised in the name of the Holy Trinity and the faith of the Church."

The rumours of the king's conversion had probably brought a vast multitude of strangers to the city, not only from other parts of Kent, but also from distant quarters. We cannot doubt that, as in the case of the baptism of Clovis, the ceremony was performed with much pomp, to impress the minds of the heathen Saxons. "On that occasion the Church was hung with embroidered tapestry and white curtains: odours of incense like airs of paradise were diffused around, and the building blazed with countless lights."

While Ethelbert remained at the entrance, Queen Bertha, with her attendants, repaired to her customary place of devotion. A portion of the service was performed at the altar, and then Augustine descended to the font, chanting a litany, and preceded by two acolytes with lighted tapers. Then followed prayers for the benediction of the font and the consecration of the water, over which Augustine makes the sign of the Cross three times. Then (according to one variation of the ancient Gallican rite) the two tapers are plunged into the font, and Augustine breathes into it (*insufflat*) three times, and the Chrism is poured into the font in the form of a Cross, while the water is parted with his hand. Ethelbert at this point is interrogated in the following simple form :— "Dost thou believe in God the Father Almighty? Dost thou too believe in Jesus Christ, His only-begotten Son, our Lord, who was born and suffered! and Dost thou believe in the

Holy Ghost, the Holy Church, the remission of sins, and
the Resurrection of the flesh?" To each of which questions
the king answers, "*I believe.*"

Here follows the actual *baptism*, after which Ethelbert
is signed on the forehead with Chrism in the form of a Cross.
Augustine returns to his seat, and another litany is chanted.
Had Augustine been at that time a bishop, he would now
have administered to the king the Sacrament of Confirmation,
but he was not consecrated bishop of the English till a few
months afterwards.

It has indeed been objected that the ceremony could not
have taken place in St. Martin's Church, because at that time
baptism was administered by immersion. This was indeed
the general rule, and such expressions as being "let down
into the water," "stepping forth from the bath," "coming
up from the font," and so on, occur in the writings of Tertullian, Jerome, the Gelasian and Leontine Sacramentaries :
and octagonal or circular baptisteries are found in ancient
churches, sometimes as much as twenty feet in diameter and
five feet deep, erected for this purpose.

On the other hand, this practice was by no means universal,
and even as early as the second century *affusion* was frequently
used, with or without immersion. A picture of our Lord's
baptism in the baptistery of St. John's at Ravenna (about 450)
represents Jesus as standing in the water, and the Baptist
pouring water over him from a shell. There is a similar representation in the church of St. Maria in Cosmedin (about 550),
and one of earlier date in a fresco from the cemetery of St.
Callixtus. On two sarcophagi, mentioned by Ciampinus, repre-
sentations of a like character are engraved, supposed to be the
Baptism of Agilulfus and Theodolinda (about 590), and of
Arrichius, second Duke of Beneventum (591). In the latter
case a man somewhat advanced in years, kneels to receive
baptism, which is administered by *affusion* only. Both of these
are assigned to the same decade as that of King Ethelbert.
We may conclude, therefore, that both forms of administering
the rite were practised from early times, and it is by no means
impossible that Ethelbert was baptised by *affusion*. It was
probably not from the existing font, even though in the
seal of N. de Battail, Abbot of St. Augustine's (1224-1252)
and in the common seal of St. Augustine's Abbey, the king is

represented as standing in a font, resembling in many respects the present one—while the baptism of Rollo, the first Christian Duke of Normandy, is illustrated in an early MS. of the twelfth-century Chronicle of Beuvit de St. More, with Rollo standing (or sitting) naked in a similar tub-like font.

St. Martin's, "a small and mean church," as it is unkindly called by Stukely, after the death of Augustine, Ethelbert, and Bertha, relapses into comparative obscurity, and its history is gathered chiefly from the testimony of architecture. We may, however, mention, as connected with the immediately succeeding period, that there were dug up in the churchyard (besides the Roman ornaments already described) a Saxon or Frankish circular ornament set with garnets, and other things which were of too costly a description to have belonged to any but persons of distinction, with whom they had probably been interred—also three gold looped Merovingian coins, fully described by Mr Roach Smith.

The first historical post-Augustinian record that we find in connection with the church is the well-known charter of 867 (from the Cottonian MSS. Augustus II. 95) granted, when the Kentish Wittenagemot was held at Canterbury, by King Ethelred, and entitled "Grant of a *sedes* in the place which is called St. Martin's Church, and of a small enclosure pertaining to the same *sedes* by King Ethelred to his faithful friend Wighelm, priest," endorsed in a contemporary hand, "An sett æt sc'e Martine." In this document Ethelred, King of the West Saxons and Kentishmen, gives and concedes to Wighelm a *sedes* and *tun* or enclosure pertaining thereto, of which the boundaries are named, but the Latin is very provincial and obscure. The grant is given to Wighelm for his life, and after his death to his heirs, and the king in strong language lays injunction on his successors "by the faith of St. Martin, confessor of Christ," not to presume to infringe the grant.

Now this charter is one of the most remarkable in the whole series of Anglo-Saxon documents, and confessedly one of the most difficult to comprehend, especially as to the word *sedes*, which is variously interpreted to refer to the episcopal character of St. Martin's, or to some official appointment in the church, or to a shop, dwelling, or stall for market purposes, in the parish. Whatever be the meaning of many difficult expressions, the charter is important as giving what is probably a complete list of the Canterbury clergy, all of whom attested it.

Archbishop . Ceolnoth.
Abbot . . Biarnhelm.
Archdeacons . Sigefred, Bearnoth, Herefreth.
Priests . . Nothheard, Biarnfreth, &c. &c. &c.

It is also attested by King Ethelred, Duke Eastmund, Abbot Ealhheard, and many others, and is confirmed "in Jesus Christ with the sign of the Holy Cross" in the year 867.

We can hardly doubt that the church suffered some injury at the hands of the Danes, by whom Canterbury was wasted in 851 and again in 1009, though the most serious devastation took place in 1011, when, in the reign of Ethelred the Second-the Danes laid siege to, and captured, the city. On that occasion Archbishop Elphege was seized, bound, and dragged to the Cathedral to see it in flames. He was then carried off, and eventually murdered at Greenwich.

Not very long after this period we discover mention of the suffragan "Bishops of St. Martin's," who were evidently *Chorepiscopi*, an ancient order of bishops, dating from the third century, who overlooked the country district committed to them, ordaining readers, exorcists and subdeacons, but not (as a rule) deacons and priests, except by express permission of the diocesan bishop. It has been wrongly supposed, without any evidence or tradition, that the bishops of St. Martin's belonged to the great church at Dover, or the Oratory of St. Martin at Romney.

It is said by Battely that the succession of these bishops lasted for the space of nearly four hundred years; but of this there is no proof, and the idea may have sprung from the charter which we have discussed above, while the actual tradition is first mentioned in the "Black Book of the Archdeacons of Canterbury" (probably compiled in the fourteenth or fifteenth century), wherein it is said that "In the time of St. Augustine, first Archbishop of Canterbury, to the time of Archbishop Lanfranc of blessed memory, there was no archdeacon in the city and diocese of Canterbury. But from the time of Archbishop Theodore, who was sixth from St. Augustine, to the time of the aforesaid Lanfranc, there was in the church of St. Martin's, a suburb of Canterbury, a bishop ordained by Theodore, under the authority of Pope Vitalian, who in all the city and diocese of Canterbury undertook duties in the place of the archbishop, conferring holy orders, consecrating churches, and confirming children during his absence." Archbishop Parker speaks of the Bishop of St. Martin's as performing in all things the office of a bishop in the absence of the archbishop, who, for the most part, attended the king's court. "The bishop, himself being a monk, received under obedience the monks of Christ Church, and celebrated in the Metropolitical Church the solemn offices of Divine worship, which being finished he returned to his own place. He and the Prior of Christ Church sat together in synods, both habited alike."

The names of only two bishops are preserved to us—that of *Eadsi* or *Eadsige* (1032-38), subsequently Archbishop of Canterbury, who, soon after he had received the pall from the Pope, was afflicted with a loathsome disease which incapacitated him for a time; though he afterwards recovered and administered the see until his death on the fourth day before the Kalends of November in 1050. The other Bishop was *Godwin*, appointed in 1052 by Archbishop Robert of Jumiéges, who died, according to the Saxon Chronicle, in 1061. The Bishop of St. Martin's was practically merged into the Archdeacon of Canterbury in the time of Lanfranc, who refused to ordain another bishop, saying that "there ought not to be two bishops in one city."

After the Conquest, St. Martin's was partially restored by the Normans, and the interior of the church underwent considerable alteration in the thirteenth century.

The list of the rectors is given in an appendix. They were not persons of any distinction, but from time to time we glean a few interesting details concerning them.

Thus, for instance, in 1321, a dispute arose between *Robert de Henney*, rector of St. Martin's, and Randolph de Waltham, master of the Free Grammar School of the city of Canterbury, about the rights and privileges of their respective schools. A Special Commission was appointed by the Archbishop, including the chaplain of St. Sepulchre's, the vicar of St. Paul's, the rector of St. Mary de Castro, rector of St. Peter's, and others. The point of dispute was whether in the St. Martin's School (within the church fence or boundary) there should be more than thirteen *grammar* scholars. The rector was limited to this number for fear of infringing on the privilege of the City Grammar School, though he was entitled to take as many scholars in reading and singing as he pleased. In fact, however, the rector took as many grammar boys as he could get, it being necessary only that when his school was visited by the city schoolmaster or his deputy, the surplus should conceal themselves for the time being. An injunction, however, was granted in the Archbishop's Court to restrain the rector from taking more than his bare thirteen.

This is an extremely interesting record, because it shows that there were two flourishing public schools in Canterbury, probably the most ancient Grammar Schools in England, early in the fourteenth century ; and that the pupils *paid* for their teaching, and learnt other subjects besides grammar.

Thorn, the monk of St. Augustine's, tells us also an amusing story of how *John de Bourne*, rector of St. Martin's, aided in the escape of one Peter de Dene from St. Augustine's Monastery by placing ladders against the monastery walls. They then rode on horseback together to Bishopsbourne, but Peter was at length recaptured.

In the fourteenth century we find no less than three rectors who were instituted to St. Martin's by the Prior of Christ Church during a vacancy in the see of Canterbury.

We have already mentioned the difficulty of obtaining information concerning the church in the Middle Ages, owing to its being exempt from the jurisdiction of the Archdeacon of Canterbury, and therefore not included in the Archidiaconal Registers, while the Archbishop's Visitations of the diocese were not, as a rule, parochial. By a lucky chance, however, we find some entries in Archbishop Warham's Visitation in 1511, one of which is to the effect that the churchwardens had not furnished accounts for five years, though they had received various monies for keeping graves in order. They were ordered to furnish accounts before the Feast of Purification, under pain of excommunication, &c.

There are many details of interest to be found in the pre-Reformation wills of parishioners, which are preserved in the "Consistory Court." In them we find bequests to the Light of the Holy Cross, the Light of the Blessed Mary, the Light of St. Martin, the Light of St. Christopher, the Light of St.

Erasmus, for daily masses before the image of St. Nicholas, to the High Altar, for the purchase of a new Cross, for various ornaments, for paving,—together with tenements, real estate, legacies for the benefit of the poor, and sundry curious personal gifts which wonderfully illustrate the habits and customs of the period. And from an inventory of Parish Church goods in Kent, made in 1552, we find the following entry relating to St. Martin's under the head of "19th July vi., Edward vi.":—

Bartylemewe Barham gent. and Stevyn Goodhewe, church-wardens.

Ffirst, one chalys with the paten of sylver.

Item, one vestment of blewe velvett with a cope to the same.

Item, one vestment of whyte braunchyd damaske with a cope to the same.

Item, one other olde vestment with a cope to the same.

Item, two table clothes.

Item, one long towell, one short towell.

Item, ij corporas with their clothes.

Item, one velvet cushon and one saten cushon.

Item, ij chysts, iiij surplysys.

Item, iij bells and one waggerell bell in the steple. Whereof left in the churche for the mynystracion of dyvyne service : The chalys with the paten of sylver, one cope of blewe velvett, one cope of whyte braunchyd damaske, ij albes, ij table clothes, one long towell, and one short towell, iiij surplysys, the bells in the steple.

For any further particulars concerning the Church after the Reformation we may refer to the meagre account given by William Somner, and the additions made to his history by Nicholas Battely, who states that " St. Martin's claims the priority in the catalogue of Canterbury parish churches upon several titles of antiquity and dignity." He says that he cannot pretend that the present fabric is the same building which was erected in or near the days of King Lucius, or which was repaired and fitted up for Queen Bertha. " But yet it has at this day the appearance of ancientness, not from the wrinkles and ruins of old age, but from the materials (*i.e.* Roman bricks) used in the repairing or re-edifying of it." He then goes on to make the erroneous statement that "in the porch of this church were buried Queen Bertha, and Liudhard, Bishop of Senlis, and (Thorn saith) King Ethelbert." About

ninety years after the time of Battely we come to a description
of the church in the pages of Hasted, who, without assign-
ing any reason, ventures on the suggestion that "the *Chancel*
was the whole of the original building of this church or
oratory, and was probably built about the year 200 : that is,
about the middle space of time when the Christians, both
Britons and Romans, lived in this island free from all
persecutions." Hasted's history is, as a rule, extremely
valuable, not only from the style of his writing, but from his
extraordinary general accuracy, and the minuteness of his
original researches : and we are often at a loss to imagine
from what source he could have derived so much information,
which at that period was not so accessible as at present.

Gostling, a minor canon of the cathedral, writes also at the
end of the last century ("Walks in and about Canterbury"),
but he adds nothing fresh except that "if the church was
larger and more magnificent (as Mr Battely seems to believe)
this might tempt the Danish invaders to make a ruin of that,
but they had no provocation here!" and he calls it elsewhere
"an obscure chapel."

It is probable that the church was much neglected during
the last, and the first forty years of the present, century.
Its existence was almost forgotten by the public at large. From
an historical edifice it sank into the insignificance of a small
parish church in a small village. It was the *site* of great
events, but only a site : and its condition is faithfully described
in some verses beneath an old print now hanging in the
vestry.

> " A humble church recalls the scenes of yore
> To present memory, yet humbled more
> By lapse of years, by lack of reverent care,
> And ill-advised expedients for repair.
> Oh ! would this age its taste and bounty blend,
> The faults of bygone ages to amend !
> And lib'rally adorn this lowly pile
> Where sleeps the first Queen Christian of our isle."

ST. MARTIN'S CHURCH (in 1840).

(From a Water-colour Drawing.)

CHAPTER III

WE come now to a description of the church, which consists of a rectangular *Nave*, 38 ft. long by 25 ft. wide; a *Chancel* (in its present form) 40 ft. by 14 ft.; a tower built in the fourteenth century, and a modern organ chamber and vestry.

The chancel originally was not as large as it is now, and probably extended only 18 or 20 ft. from the present chancel arch. An external buttress on the south side marks its termination, beyond which it has been conjectured that there was an Eastern apse, as sketched in the annexed plan.

The first question that naturally suggests itself is with regard to the **Dedication.** Battely, followed by Hasted, was of opinion that the church was originally dedicated to the Blessed Virgin Mary, and afterwards re-dedicated to St. Martin by Bishop Liudhard. For this statement there is apparently no authority, yet we must remember that the earliest dedications of churches were either to the Saviour, the Blessed Virgin, or one of the twelve Apostles. That the Italian Mission followed generally this ancient practice is shown in their dedication of the cathedrals of Canterbury, Rochester, London, and York to Christ, St. Andrew, St. Paul, and St. Peter respectively—of St. Augustine's Abbey church to St. Peter and St. Paul, of another church in the same abbey to the "Holy Mother of God," and also of the early Saxon church in Lyminge to St. Mary; but it is unnecessary to multiply further instances, the very rare exceptions to the rule (such as St. Pancras) applying principally to churches which contained the relics of martyrs. This exception would not embrace St. Martin's—and Battely's statement, therefore, from whatever source he derived it, is not intrinsically impossible. We can say nothing more positive in its favour—but assuming it to be true, and that the original dedication

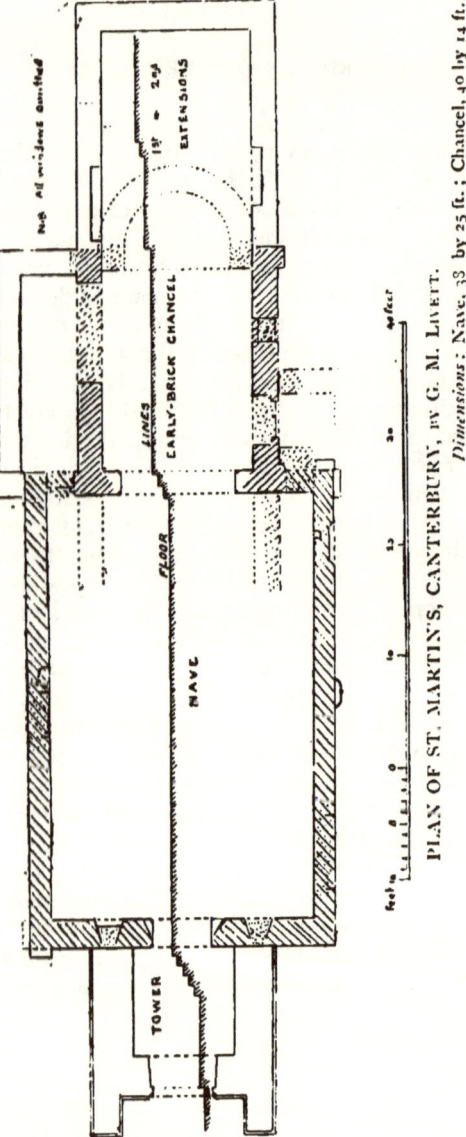

PLAN OF ST. MARTIN'S, CANTERBURY, by G. M. LIVETT.

Dimensions: Nave, 38 by 25 ft.; Chancel, 40 by 14 ft.

was forgotten, nothing would be more natural than that the re-dedication of the church should be to the saintly Bishop of Tours, made either by Germanus in 429, or Bishop Liudhard, or even Augustine himself. It is marvellous how widespread was the influence of St. Martin's name. Nearly 4000 churches are dedicated to him in France alone, and the largest number of these (in a comparison of dioceses) is in the part of France nearest to English shores.

But, supposing we take literally the words of Bede, that the church "dedicated to the honour of St. Martin, was built of old, while the Romans still occupied Britain," we are met by this apparent difficulty. If (as is maintained) the church was built in the fourth century, how came it to be dedicated to St. Martin, who died about 397 ? Some colourable support to the possibility of this can be derived from the fact that the first stone church built in Scotland (at Whithern) by St. Ninian was certainly dedicated to the same saint. There are indeed, in that case, some special reasons, because St. Ninian, a personal friend of St. Martin, called on him at Tours, and received from him workmen accustomed to the Roman method of building, with whom he returned home. As the church was in course of erection, the news of St. Martin's death reached him, and the church was in consequence dedicated in 398 to his memory. There need be no difficulty on the doubtfulness of such an early *Canonization*. The first formal act of canonization by a Pope did not take place till the ninth or tenth century. Before this, it was done in a somewhat irregular manner by the bishop of the diocese, who recited the names of the departed martyrs, or holy men, in the *Canon* of the mass, not for invocation, but in memory of those who had finished their course, and for an example to others. It has been asserted that St. Martin was the first person to be honoured as a confessor, that is, that he was the first who was treated as a saint without being a martyr. In the antiphon to the Magnificat on his festival we have, "sanctissima anima, quam etsi gladius persecutoris non abstulit, palmam tamen martyrii non amisit." Though there were *other* St. Martins, such as the Bishop of Vienne, a Bishop of Tongres at the end of the third century, and a Bishop of Trèves, yet there can be little doubt that the one alluded to by Bede was the Bishop of Tours, whose fame had completely overshadowed the rest.

Now there is one suggestion that deserves a passing notice, and that is, the possibility of St. Martin himself having been the founder of the church; even in a closer sense than by merely sending masons from his monastery, as he did to St. Ninian. In the constant interchange of communication between Britain and Gaul, not only for commercial but for military purposes, it may have happened that Christians had migrated, or been transferred, from Tours to Kent- and for the benefit of Christian soldiers, St. Martin, once a soldier himself, may have urged the erection of a church. It is unnatural to suppose that St. Martin, who travelled over a great part of Gaul, did not in some way associate himself with Britons, with whom he would have been brought into contact. We know this, at anyrate, that during the latter year of his episcopate he exercised great influence over the Emperor Maximus and his Empress—and Maximus had resided for several years in Britain, was proclaimed emperor there in 383, had thence invaded Gaul with a fleet and army, which were long afterwards remembered as the "emigration of a considerable part of the British nation," and finally settled at Trèves, where he was more than once visited by St. Martin. Some of these British emigrants or soldiers would very naturally have returned to their native country and brought Christianity with them. There is no conclusive reason why St. Martin himself, either prompted thereto by Maximus, or yielding to the entreaties of Britons whom he met at Trèves or elsewhere in Gaul, should not have visited Canterbury in person, and there founded the church. It is remarked by Haddan and Stubbs that "it was a peculiarity of British Christians that churches were not dedicated to any saint already dead, after the fashion then beginning to be common, but were called by the name of their living founder." Or the original dedication made by St. Martin (acting either directly or indirectly) may have fallen into popular disuse, and been supplanted by his own name, as was the case with the church of St. Gregory on the Cœlian Hill, which St. Gregory had dedicated to St. Andrew, but which soon after came to be called after himself, though he was not buried there. And attention may be directed to instances of a similar kind at Rome, where the names of founders lingered on in churches like the Basilica Constantiniana, Basilica Liberiana, and St. Lorenzo in Damaso. We may also note the fact, that a chapel in Canterbury Cathedral, originally dedicated to St. Peter and St. Paul, soon acquired the name of its founder, St. Anselm, and even the great Cathedral itself, the "Church of Christ," was popularly known in the Middle Ages as the Church of St. Thomas. These latter instances are not indeed exactly parallel, because the relics of the name-saints were actually buried in these places, but they may be quoted as showing how readily the original dedication may have been subsequently changed; and it would not be difficult to give additional examples.

Before proceeding to a minute description of the principal objects of interest outside the church, we may say a few words about the **walls,** which, however, have been so patched and repaired in successive ages, that they have lost all signs of uniformity. The thickness of the walls is, on an average, about 2 ft., and this dimension is noticeable, because we meet with it over and over again in Roman villas. The materials, too, are similar, and resemble what have been found in villas—a mass of rather rough walling, partly of brick, partly of stone, evidently intended to be plastered on both sides, and, to a great extent, built with hard "sea-shore" mortar. This mortar is composed of pebbles, small shells, etc., and is of such remarkable solidity and strength that, although the walls of the church are thin and lofty, they have sustained without any injury, and with comparatively low buttresses, the thrust of a high-pitched Gothic roof. It was not uncommon for churches to be erected on the site of, and using part of the structure of, Roman secular buildings, or temples. And we give for what it is worth the opinion of Mr Roach Smith, an experienced antiquary, who gave special attention to Roman work, and who states in a letter written on January 6, 1883 : "There are many examples of churches being built upon the remains of Roman buildings, no doubt often *temples*, and not unfrequently of a small size. Some instances are very remarkable, as that of Britford, near Salisbury, at old Verulam, etc. I have ever had a belief that St. Martin's Church is founded upon, or built upon, or built into, a Roman temple."

The walls of the church form an interesting study, not only for their venerable aspect, but also for their irregularity. The brick courses in the **Nave** are pretty general throughout, sometimes at 9 inches apart, sometimes as much as 20 inches, or even more. A great deal of old plaster is found externally in the middle of the south wall of the *nave*, and there are masses of Roman bricks congregated at the east and west ends of the same wall (the angles of the walls in public buildings being often composed entirely of bricks); and we find also, in parts, large blocks of grey stone, as well as pieces of travertine, tertiary sandstone, Kentish rag, red sandstone, Purbeck marble, chalk, and many other geological specimens. Here and there, interspersed with Roman bricks, are patches of "chequy" masonry, the stones being placed at wide intervals, notably on the south-east corner, and on the north side.

The masonry of the early **chancel** is, however, entirely different, being composed of Roman bricks laid evenly upon one another with narrow joints, averaging four bricks to a foot. In many instances the arrises of these bricks are sharp and true, showing no sign of having been taken from any other building; in other cases they are more fragmentary, but we can have no hesitation in saying that the walling of the early chancel is well-built, satisfactory to a professional eye.

We have then these two distinct modes of building (1) Roman bricks laid evenly and closely upon one another, (2) stone-work with courses of Roman brick at various intervals. And we shall have to consider hereafter whether these are genuine Roman walls, or are merely composed of Roman materials used up for the second time, as at St. Albans and elsewhere.

We learn from competent authorities that there were five or six kinds of Roman wall-building—(*a*) The *quadrangular*, with masses of square or oblong stones laid alternately lengthwise and cross-wise, not cemented by mortar, but bound together by leaden clamps, such as is found in the so-called wall of Romulus on the Palatine ; (*b*) *polygonal* masonry, where the stones are irregular, and with small stone splinters wedged into the joints where necessary ; (*c*) *concrete*-rude, without ornamentation, which has at a distance the appearance of being panelled, since beams of timber are let in to strengthen it, or sometimes thin layers of brick to prevent settlement in the concrete from the shrinking of the lime when it cools and dries ; (*d*) *opus reticulatum*, which consists of stone net-work of diamond-shaped blocks, as in the "Muro Torto" at Rome ; (*e*) *opus lateritium*, the ordinary construction of bricks laid

evenly upon one another ; (*f*) *mixture—i.e.* stones bonded together with courses of bricks, sometimes at regular, often at
irregular, intervals. Mr Parker, in his "Archæology of Rome,"
referring to the *mixture* (*i.e.* the style of the building used in
the nave) which is so constant in Roman wall-work, in England
and Northern Europe generally, says that in itself it is no
evidence of date as to the period of Roman work, since other
things must be taken into account : but that it is found in the
circus of Maxentius, and many other places.   It is usually
attributed to the beginning of the fourth century, but it occurs
also at Pompeii, in parts of the substructure of the walls of
Aurelian, in tombs of the second century at Ostia, and in some
of the foundations of Hadrian's villa near Tivoli.

With regard to the comparative antiquity of the nave and
chancel, no positive judgment has yet been arrived at.
Hasted, indeed, ventured on the opinion that the latter
was the more ancient, but he also believed that the chancel
was built about the year 200 A.D., and had not the benefit of
the recent explorations, so that his opinion is, in itself, of
little value.   But it has been adopted on scientific and
architectural grounds by the Rev. G. M. Livett (who has
paid careful attention to the architecture and masonry of
the church) and by other distinguished antiquaries.   Their
arguments are very forcible, and there is much reason for
believing that the theory will hereafter find general acceptance,
although at present further investigation is necessary before
it can be pronounced as incontrovertible.

We know indeed that some of the earliest Roman buildings
were constructed of Roman bricks or tiles laid evenly upon
one another (the *opus lateritium*), but the tiles of the first
two centuries were remarkably thin, as contrasted with later
specimens. They vary, at different periods, in length from
15 inches to 2 feet, and in thickness from ¾ inch to 3 inches.
Unfortunately little credence is now given to the ingenious
rough-and-ready rule, formulated by Mr Parker, that where
(including mortar) there are ten bricks to one foot, the
wall is of the *first* century, as in the arches of Nero; where
eight bricks, of the *second* century, as in the villa of Hadrian ;
where six bricks, of the *third* century, as in Aurelian's wall ;
where four bricks, of the *fourth* century. We may lament
the non-acceptance of this rule, for, were it true, we might

confidently assign the early wall of the chancel (containing four bricks to a foot) to the *fourth* century, which is the exact date that is claimed for it!

With regard to the **foundations**, those in the chancel are of flint-stones and mortar, with a footing of a single course of Roman bricks, while in the nave we find a mixture of sandy mortar and crushed flint, topped with courses of Kentish rag-stone, and one or sometimes two courses of brick.

Closely connected with the walls are the **buttresses**. Of flat pilaster buttresses there are at the present moment (*a*) one on the south side of the chancel; (*b*) two at the south-east corner of the nave, at right angles to each other; (*c*) one at the north-west corner of the nave, the corresponding buttress at this place having been cut away. In addition to these, there is an evidently later one on the north-east of the nave, and a semi-circular buttress in the middle of the south wall. They have all been repaired very frequently, especially at the top, and it is difficult to determine which stones are original, and which have been inserted afterwards. The sole remaining buttress in the chancel has been mutilated in a painful manner. Not so many years ago, before the modern quoins of Caen stone were added, it was largely composed of Roman bricks similar to the walling. The other flat buttresses on the south side project 6 inches from the wall, and, as we see them at present, consist of blocks of rough-hewn Caen stone to the height of 4 ft. 6 in., and, above that, of Roman brick, considerably patched.

In themselves flat pilaster buttresses furnish no evidence as to date, since they are found alike in Roman, Saxon, and Norman buildings. It is contended by Mr Livett that the buttresses in the nave are Norman, or (at anyrate) insertions of a later date than the adjacent wall—but only those at the south-east angle have been explored, where the foundations seem to be of a whiter, harder mortar than those of the wall, containing large stones, but no small angular flints. It is too early as yet to pronounce any positive opinion on the point.

Special attention has often been called to the semi-circular buttress, because this shape is uncommon, though something like it is found at St. Peter's, Northampton, at the Church of St. Remi at Rheims, and elsewhere. The outstanding portion of it measures almost exactly three feet in circumference. It cannot have been made (as some have supposed) to contain a staircase, because there seems no reason whatever for a staircase at this particular place, the rood-loft being several feet eastwards. Others have conjectured that

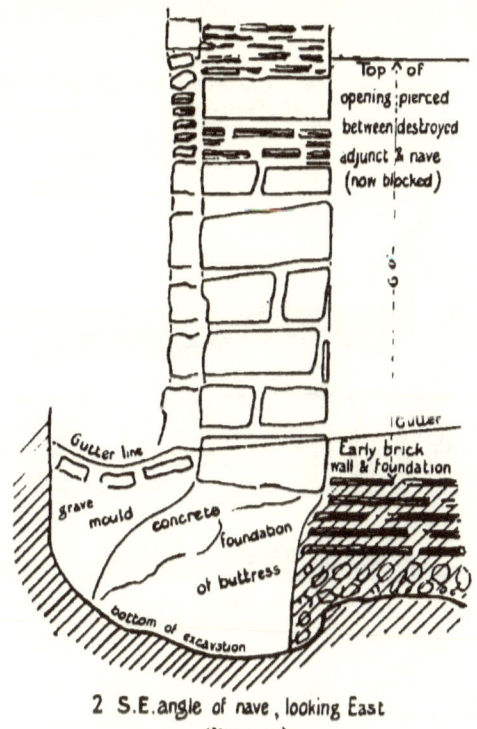

2 S.E. angle of nave, looking East
(Buttress.)

the old church might have ended somewhere near this point, and that then the buttress would have had something to do with the support of the western front, or have been a staircase up to the old belfry. But there is no foundation for this surmise, which is disproved by the fact that the external plaster extends on each side of the buttress, and the character of the south wall is absolutely unbroken. This external plaster, indeed, is probably not Roman, though it

D

is composed to some extent of pounded brick. The buttress
bears little or no resemblance to the lofty semi-circular
projection occasionally found in Saxon towers. Its object
must be left in a state of obscurity, and it may perhaps have
been a mere freak of the builder.

At a distance of 10 ft. 6 in. from this circular buttress
we come to a *nearly circular panel*, immediately behind the

St Martins Church near Canterbury where K: Ethelberts Queen us'd to go to Christian Service

Erudito viro et Amicissimo John Hardy de Nottingham
Tabulam hanc erexit W. Stukley
Date 1722.

Norman piscina, which has always been a puzzle to antiquaries.
The dimensions of it, as now seen, are roughly 4 ft. by 3 ft.
8 in. It is sunk 6 in. into the wall, is unevenly splayed, and
in parts plastered. In Stukely's engraving of the church
(1722 A.D.) it is represented as a round-headed doorway, but
there are no voussoirs or arch stones. The result of excavations beneath the surface are doubtful. Generally speaking,
there are courses of two Roman bricks running along this
part of the nave wall, below which are Kentish rag stones,
and a foundation of concrete. Singularly enough, the *top*
row of Roman bricks (just below the opening) has been

interrupted for a space of 3 ft. 8 in., and it looks at first sight as if the *lower* row were the sill of a doorway, from which a slight suspicion of a rough vertical joint goes upwards for a little distance. But against this theory we must state that the *one-brick* course does not extend the whole width of the panel. The immediate back of the Norman piscina was discovered on investigation, not to be of stone, as we might have expected, but of coarse thin plaster, and it is not impossible that this back was taken out sometime in the Early English period, and that the opening thus made was used as a hagioscope. No plausible theory has been advanced as to the use of this *panel*. It was once suggested that it was a niche for a churchyard-light, which would shine on the south side of the church. This, sometimes consisting of a covered lamp, would be used to light at night the mortuary convoys that came from afar, and could not always arrive in the daytime. It was also a sort of homage rendered to the memory of the dead, a signal recalling to passers-by the presence of the departed, and inviting prayers for them. But this is entirely a fanciful idea.

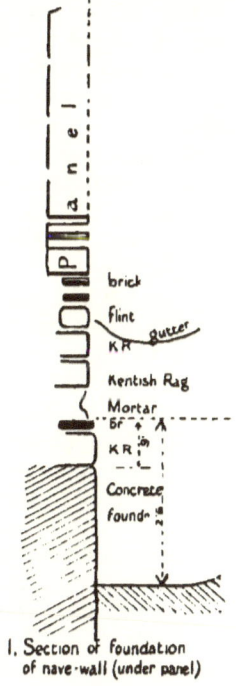

I. Section of foundation of nave-wall (under panel)

The **doorways** are the next feature of interest. With them St. Martin's is extremely well supplied, as (counting both ancient and modern ones) there are no less than six, though they were doubtless not all used at the same period. It would seem as if the architects of one age found a positive pleasure in blocking up and replacing doorways of preceding ages ! At the south-west corner of the nave, immediately outside the font, is an Early English doorway or porch, seven feet wide, probably built in the thirteenth century, and now closed up with blocks of chalk, in the middle of which is inserted part of a two-light window. This may have been substituted for the usual Saxon "south-door." On the north side of the nave there are also traces of an Early English porch, which was only taken down during the present century within the memory of persons still living. The peculiarity of this porch is that it was added on to what we believe to be an older Norman doorway, which will be spoken of when we describe the interior of the church.

Proceeding to the south side of the chancel and its adjacent portion of the east wall of the nave, we come upon three curious openings. Two of them are square-headed. (1) The one at the south-east corner of the nave is 6 ft. high, and splayed externally, being 2 ft. 8 in. wide inside, and 3 ft. wide outside the church. It has a lintel and threshold of Roman brick, and has been blocked up with masses of chalk and rubble. The plaster on the splays is still *in situ*, and was considered, at a meeting of the British Archæological Society, to be "most probably Roman." But it has been clearly demonstrated that it is a later insertion in the wall. Its position at the east angle of the nave is very peculiar, and its use has not yet been ascertained. At the beginning of the extensive explorations that have been lately carried out, when it was believed by some antiquaries that there was a *Western apse* similar to that in the Christian church at Silchester, and that the arch (described hereafter) was the opening into this apse, this south-eastern doorway was supposed to have been one of the entrances either to the church, or the *Narthex* (vestibule), there being some indications of a corresponding doorway in the north-eastern angle of the nave. This theory appears to be now generally abandoned, but it is quite possible that it may be revived when further excavations are made beneath the tower. (2) The other opening at the south-west of the chancel, 6 ft. high and 3 ft. 4 in. wide externally, has jambs of Roman bricks, with a lintel and sill formed of massive blocks of green sandstone, much worn by weather. Internally it seems 4 ft. 7 in. at the top, but this may be accounted for by the fact that in later times it was partially blocked up by a stone sarcophagus, and other material : and on one side of the upper portion of the doorway, and extending beyond it towards the west, there was opened a low side-window, the western splayed jamb of which is still remaining, with the original plaster. This may perhaps have been a "Lepers' window" commanding a view of the altar of St. Mary, occupying the

S.-W. EXTERIOR OF CHANCEL.　　(From a Water-colour by Mrs. M. Parry.)

site of the present pulpit. This square-headed doorway is
certainly contemporaneous with the surrounding wall. When
it was first exposed, we found in it the skeleton of a sparrow !

Near these square-headed doorways there were discovered
underground the remains of two walls, running at right angles
to the chancel, and forming two sides of an *adjunct* or side
chapel, the southern side of which has been destroyed in
the process of digging graves. These walls are 4 ft. 9 in.
apart, and are each of them 26 in. wide, built entirely of

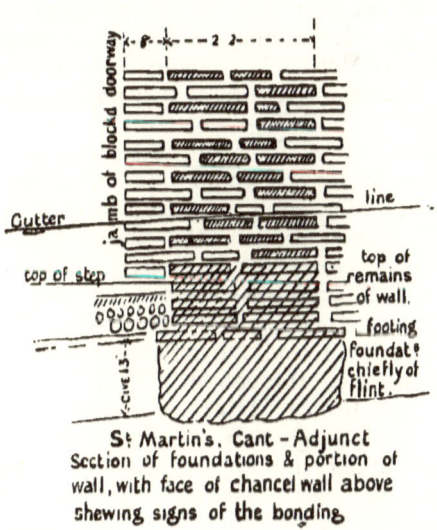

St Martin's. Cant – Adjunct
Section of foundations & portion of
wall, with face of chancel wall above
shewing signs of the bonding

Roman bricks. The western wall runs eight inches beneath
the eastern angle-wall of the nave. Between the walls there is
still existing part of a flooring of *opus signinum*. There can
be no doubt that this *adjunct* is of the same workmanship, and
the same date, as the early brick wall of the chancel. The
foundations of both are precisely similar, and are constructively
bonded together—the walls rest upon a footing-course of one
brick, which forms the top of a shallow foundation of flints and
stones. The brick-footing is continued along the chancel wall
under the sill of the square-headed doorway, and is irregular in
its projection. A careful examination of the existing face of
the chancel wall above the remains (which was made by Mr

Livett), shows that the eastern wall of the *adjunct* above
ground, now destroyed, was originally bonded into the chancel
wall. Every alternate course shows a broken brick, and every
intermediate course the clean edge of a brick. This bonding
cannot be traced above a line on a level with the lower edge
of the lintel of the square-headed doorway of the chancel.

What the purpose of this *adjunct* was, we cannot positively
determine. It was suggested by the late Archbishop of
Canterbury (who took the warmest interest in the church, and
also keenly watched the progress of the excavations) that it
was used as a place for baking the holy bread employed at the
celebration of the Mass. It is more probable, however, notwithstanding its diminutive size, that it was a side-chapel with
its altar.

At a distance of 4 ft. 2 in. eastwards of the square-
headed doorway is a *semi-circular* one. It is 6 ft. high and
2 ft. 1 in. wide. The arch is mostly formed of converging
blocks of Kentish rag, generally about one inch apart,
though somewhat closer at the crown. The span at the
springing is an inch or two wider than the span of the jambs.
The imposts are formed of two Roman tiles, the upper one
overhanging the lower, and the lower overhanging the jamb.
The doorway is lined throughout with plaster. The jambs
internally are of Roman bricks with occasional pieces of
Kentish rag. *Externally*, they are almost entirely of Roman
bricks, though under the west impost, 3 ft. 10 in. above
the sill, there has been inserted a fragment of freestone
about 2½ inches high, brought from elsewhere. On
this are parts of an inscription, which has been supposed
by many people to date from the ninth or tenth century,
though this date cannot be accepted as proved. The letters
HONORE . . ST.E . . ET OMNIV̄ SC̄ORV̄ are still decipher-
able, and the whole may perhaps be read as "To the
honour of Saint (Mary?) and All Saints." This may have
been the dedication-stone of a church, or not impossibly
the dedication-stone of an altar, as an order was issued
in the ninth century by a Saxon archbishop, that a stone
should be placed at the corner of each altar, specifying the
name of the saint or saints to whom it was dedicated. A
parallel to this has been found in the discovery of a stone
from the Saxon Church of Deerhurst, the fragmentary in-

SAXON DOORWAY IN CHANCEL (INTERIOR).

(From a Drawing by Mrs M. Parry.)

scription on which has been conjecturally read as " In honore Sanctæ Trinitatis hoc altare dedicatum est."

This round-headed doorway has been hitherto supposed to be of the same date as the wall, but closer investigation has clearly proved that it is a later insertion, probably made in the

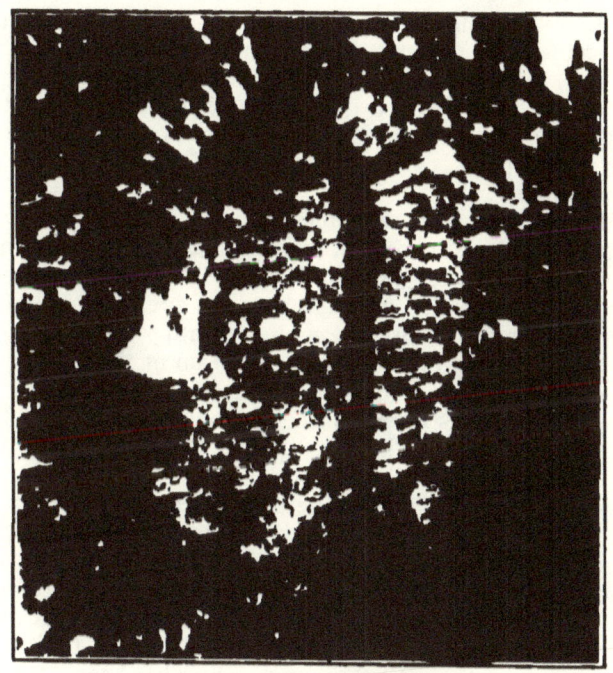

SAXON DOORWAY (EXTERIOR).

(From a Photograph by the Author.)

Saxon period, possibly as early as St. Augustine. While in the surrounding wall there are *four* Roman bricks to the foot, there are in the jambs of the doorway *six* bricks to the foot : and at the time of the insertion, nearly one foot of the surrounding wall was broken away, as will be noticed by any experienced observer.

At 4 ft. 8 in. eastward of this doorway, we come to the chancel-buttress which has been already described. A hole has been pierced in the wall immediately east of the buttress, and a clean face of Roman brick has been traced for 26 inches, in continuation of the east face of the buttress, running therefore at right angles to the outer wall, thus clearly showing that there was no buttress on the east side of the angle of the original wall.

The whole controversy as to the existence of an Eastern apse is so interesting and important, but at the same time so technical for the ordinary reader, that we have placed, in Appendix C, a contribution which Mr Livett has kindly sent to us, with the hope that it may be extensively read and pondered by all those, whether antiquaries or otherwise, who desire to weigh every point connected with the architecture and plan of the church.

While still examining the exterior of the church, we may notice on the east wall of the present chancel a nearly square insertion, measuring $14\frac{1}{2}$ by $13\frac{1}{2}$ inches. The matrix seems to represent traces of a brass, with a kneeling female figure, carrying a child in her arms, with an inscription underneath; and it may have been connected with a tomb in that portion of the churchyard. It is of the fifteenth century, but there is no evidence of its origin, though it has probably been in its present position for a considerable period. The date of 1662, and many subsequent dates and initials, have been cut into the stone, showing the continuous existence of that pernicious class of tourists who make a point of leaving their mark in places of interest!

Passing down the north side of the church, we may observe on the chancel wall a piece of masonry, composed of Roman bricks, which is a good imitation of Roman work; next the modern vestry which has no merit except that of utility, and the traces of the Early English porch, which has been described above—and then, rounding the north-west angle, we come to a curious Norman squint or hagioscope, partially hidden by the tower. The opening, sunk some three or four inches in the outer wall, is of an oblong character. The sides are formed of worked chalk and Kentish rag, with traces of a hinge and receptacle for a bolt, while the lintel is composed of a piece of oak greatly decayed by age. The squint is partially splayed on both sides, rather more on the right side than the left, extends 18 inches into the interior of the church, and commanded apparently a view of the high altar. Whether it was a lychnoscope, or leper's window, or used by penitents standing under cover of a porch, there are no grounds for determining. The actual opening does not measure more than 12 inches by 8, and was lined originally with Norman plaster. On the inside, where it is 15 inches across, it was till recently concealed by the woodwork of a pew, but this has happily been removed. The masonry inside is of a rugged character, and was evidently disturbed when the interior of the church was covered by thick coats of plaster. Among the fillings-up of the squint, we found three curious circular stones, each with an ornamental *volute* at the end. They are of oolite, and probably formed parts of a scroll at the top of a Roman (heathen) altar, and one of the fragments had small pieces of salmon-coloured mortar adhering to it. We may refer to an opening in the church of St. Mary, in Dover Castle, as being in a somewhat similar position, but there it is generally supposed to be a lychnoscope for the use of soldiers in the guard-room, so that they might watch the light burning at the altar on the south-east of the nave, which was specially reserved for them.

There is a great difference of opinion as to the proper name of these openings, two of which are certainly, and another possibly, found in St. Martin's Church. We are told that the squint is not to be confounded with low side-windows or lychnoscopes, originally unglazed. Squints, as a rule, may be defined as inside the church, and the others outside, primarily for the purpose of enabling persons in the aisles to see the elevation of the Host at the high altar, though they are sometimes found connected with a side-chapel, a parvise, or a tower-chamber. Their usual height is about 4 ft. from the ground, extending upwards from 2 to 10 ft. Narrow at first, they were gradually enlarged and broadened, as at St. Clement's and St. Peter's churches in Sandwich. Sometimes when near a side-altar they were utilised as a credence, or had a *piscina* sunk in them (*cf.* Crawley Church in Hampshire)—and it is not impossible that the only real squint or hagioscope in St. Martin's Church was through the back of the existing piscina. The other openings, as I have said, might have been used as lepers' windows, or for penitents.

The tower was added in the fourteenth century. It is somewhat squat, and crowned with a pyramidal top. It measures 16 ft. by 13 ft. 3 in. in length and width, with two large buttresses on the west side, each projecting

4 ft. 3 in. It is built principally of flint with a slight intermixture of thin mediæval tiles, and has three louvre windows, one of which, with the peculiar "long and short" features of Saxon stone work, may have been transferred there from some other portion of the church. The building of this tower has probably destroyed some interesting feature, that stood at the west end of the original church. This may have been a western apse (so common in early basilicas) or perhaps a baptistery, or a chamber with an arch on each of its four sides. Whatever it be, is at present a matter of conjecture, but further explorations may solve the mystery ; and wise men will forbear to dogmatise, when their positive theories may at any moment be overthrown.

Description of the interior.—The gradual ascent to St. Martin's Church from the lych-gate is somewhat remarkable. After turning a sharp corner in the churchyard path, you walk up nine steps to the Western Door, and from this door there is an ascent of eleven steps to the altar. This much resembles what is so noticeable a feature in Canterbury Cathedral. On the south wall of the tower-porch there is inserted a monumental stone, about which there has been a good deal of discussion. It has been described as a piece of a Roman coffin, but this is clearly a mistake. Both the character of the inscription, and the chamfering of the upper part, not unlike the tomb of Stephen Langton in St. Michael's Chapel in the Cathedral, show that it may be attributed to the thirteenth century. The letters are fragmentary, and slightly indistinct. We can, however, make out † ᑌ ᐃ, and on the other side ᘔARISCVS. It has been suggested that this word may have been " Mariscus," and then the stone might possibly have been the boundary-stone of a marsh ; but I think there can be no doubt that it is an ordinary sepulchral slab.

Till two years ago, the first feeling of visitors to the church was one of profound disappointment. They had been informed that St. Martin's was the oldest church in England ; but the proofs of antiquity were not obvious at a casual glance, and the Early English chancel arch presented itself most obtrusively to the view, the walls of the nave, too, being covered with a thick layer of modern-looking yellowish plaster. It is rather amusing, sometimes, to hear the comments and to observe the behaviour of casual visitors. Many of them are from the United States of America, where the church is placed on the "list of sights" to be seen during their European tour. A few of the more unintelligent put their heads inside the building for two or three minutes, say to one another "this is an interesting old church," and then walk away with a proud consciousness that they have *done* St. Martin's. The present writer remembers lionising a party of Americans, and completely failing to engross their attention by any historical or antiquarian description. At last, in despair, he asked them to write their names in the visitors' book kept in the vestry, where it so happened that the last names written were those of the Duchess of Edinburgh and her children. Then their interest was at once aroused, and they went away in a state of perfect happiness because their autographs were inscribed in the same page as those of Royalty! At another time the writer was preaching a sermon, on the festival of St. Martin, bishop and confessor. He was surprised to notice an allusion to his sermon in one of the leading London newspapers on the following day, with a general tone of satisfaction that Protestant England still entertained such devotion and reverence for the great *Martin Luther*, to whom (in the correspondent's imagination) the church was dedicated! Happily such ignorance is scarcely now possible, and the stripping of the plaster from the nave, and also from the lower portion of the chancel, reveals at once the antiquity of the church, so that the attention of every one of the 10,000 tourists who annually visit it is arrested (whether they will or no) by the rough uncoated walls.

This manifest improvement has been carried out with the kind consent and cordial assistance of the Rev. L. J. White-Thomson, the present rector.

It is very difficult now to realise what the church must have looked like in the earliest times. Even its shape then has been a fierce subject of dispute. Whether the chancel was added to the nave, or the nave to the chancel, or whether there was only the present chancel extended for a considerable distance westward, we may perhaps assume, in the light of very recent inves-

tigation, that there was an original chancel arch built of Roman
bricks, not unlike the arch in St. Mary's Church at Dover Castle
—and in the small, possibly apsidal, chancel the high altar
would have stood, about 18 to 20 feet eastward of the arch.

At a later period there was a *Rood-beam* mentioned in the
" Cross Light on the Rood-loft," and alluded to in the burial of
John Hougham " before the High Cross in the Nave." The
holes made for the insertion of this Rood-beam may still be seen
in the north-east and south-east angles of the nave, about 6 ft.
distant from the joints of the chancel arch, and 10 ft. above
the ground.   It at one time occurred to us as possible that the
" High Cross in the Nave " might have had a parallel in the
great stone cross found in front of the central arch between the
nave and chancel at Reculver.   " One of the fairest and most
stately Crosses (says Leland) I ever saw — nine feet, as I
guess, in height.   It standeth like a fair column."

In mediæval times, we learn from the wills of parishioners
that there were in the church images of St. Martin, St. Mary,
St. Christopher, St. Nicholas and St. Erasmus ; and each of
them had a light burning before it.   How these images were
distributed we have no evidence to determine, but (perhaps)
they were arranged in the following manner :—Image of St.
Martin at the east end, of St. Mary and St. Nicholas in the
nave on each side of the chancel arch, and the images of St.
Christopher and St. Erasmus at the west end of the church.

The high altar, according to custom, was evidently dedicated
to St. Martin, the altar on the north-east side of the nave to
the Blessed Virgin, and that on the south-east side to St.
Nicholas.   We read that William Harry left money for a
waxlight burning before the image of St. Nicholas, " where the
priest was to sing the testator's daily mass "; and there was
a " Brotherhood of St. Nicholas," at whose cost fifteen masses
were to be said for the soul of Thomas Fayrhand (A.D. 1505).

Some astonishment may be caused, at first sight, by the
mention of *St. Erasmus*, but we learn from other sources that
he was a popular saint in England.   Some glass, for instance,
in the church of St. Botolph, Lullingstone, represents a legend
of his martyrdom, his prostrate body lying beneath a windlass,
by the winding of which the saint is being disembowelled.   He
is reported to have suffered death in the Diocletian persecution
at Formiæ, where Gregory the Great testifies that his body was

THE FONT.

E.

still remaining, though it was afterwards translated to Cajeta. Under the appellation of St. Elmo, he is still invoked by Mediterranean sailors.

Though by no means the earliest feature in point of date, yet the **Font** is the most conspicuous object to one entering the church. It stands now at the south-west corner, but, until fifty years ago, it stood in the middle of the nave. We know its exact position because Stephen Fokys or Falkes (1506) directed that he should be buried " before the font," and his gravestone, with a small brass inserted, is still remaining. This brass bears the following inscription :—" Pray for the souls of Stevyn Falkes and Alys his wife : the which deceased the 10th day of May the year of our Lord 1506. On whose souls Jesu have mercy."

The *Font* is circular or tub-shaped, 2 ft. 5 in. high, excluding the base on which it stands : or 3 ft. 1 in. with the base, which looks like an old Norman mill-stone, and was probably added when the font was moved to its present position. On examining the inside of the font a few years ago, for the purpose of inserting a small leaden pipe to carry away the baptismal water, we found that this base-stone had a square opening in the centre, and bore Norman toolmarks, which it would probably not have done had it not been originally exposed to external view. The diameter of the inner basin of the font is 1 ft. 10 in., that of the outside 2 ft. 6½ in., the circumference round the outside being 8 ft. 2 in. It consists of a rim and three tiers. The three tiers are made up of some twenty-two distinct stones, rounded externally, and fitted in their place. The *lower* tier is embellished with a continuous pattern of scroll-work : the *second* with groups of circles intertwining one another (what Hasted calls a hieroglyphical true-lover's knot), with the exception of one stone, which has six comparatively plain circles carved upon it : the *third* tier is of a different character, exhibiting arches intersecting each other. At the top is a *rim*, the ornamentation of which corresponds with that of the two lower tiers, except one part in which there is a kind of dog-tooth work, like stars cut in half. It has been suggested that the upper portion of this rim was cut away for the purpose of forming a ledge on which a tall cover might firmly rest. There are still remains of the staple by which the cover was secured, and the font may have been locked up in the time of Cromwell, to prevent its desecration.

The font was for a long time covered with a thick coat of whitewash. It is lined with lead, extending downwards to a depth of 14 inches, and the space between the lead and the bottom of the font is now filled up with rough blocks of Caen stone and rubbish. It has probably been taken to pieces and moved more than once. An attempt was made, by drawing tracings of the several stones separately, to reorganise it (on paper) in a consistent and continuous pattern, but, unfortunately, there are two or three stones that will not fit in with the rest.

Now, as to the **date of the Font**, there is great diversity of opinion. The character of the carving naturally suggests that it is of the later Norman period, and is similar to that found in St. Clement's Church, Sandwich, in the cloisters of Canterbury Cathedral, and elsewhere. But this is by no means conclusive ; for, if the font was an historical or unusually ancient one, some pious person might have been inclined to do honour to it by decoration. It may be pointed out that this decoration is not *carving* at all, but has been done with a small chisel of not more than a quarter of an inch, and by no able hand. Instances have been adduced of "smartening up" of a similar character.

It is certain that the composition of the font is most unusual. The Norman fonts were, as a rule, scooped out of a single stone, as we see, *e.g.* at Lincoln Cathedral, Sapcote, Green's Norton, Belton, Aswarly, Darenth, and several other places. Moreover, if (which is somewhat uncertain) St. Martin's font is of Caen stone, which the Normans possessed abundantly, and which is easily worked, it appears improbable that they would have built it up in such a rude manner of twenty-two separate stones   Is there any other existing font composed in the same manner ?   It was said that there is, or was, at Lewknor and at Woburn.   But the vicar of Lewknor, examining his font at our request, writes that, so far as he can see, it is made of *one* stone : while the church at Woburn has been rebuilt during the last thirty years, and no one knows what has become of the original font.   A general statement that we have no Saxon fonts existing is valueless, and incapable of proof ; and we are more inclined to agree with Mr F. A. Paley (" Introduction to

Noakes, Canterbury, Photo.]

INTERIOR OF ST. MARTIN'S (SHOWING WEST WALL OF NAVE).

Illustrations of Baptismal Fonts") that "we cannot doubt that a considerable number of fonts now exist in England, wherein the Saxon infant received the waters of baptism."

The most ancient form of fonts was octagonal, or tub-shaped, built like a tower, as described by St. Paulinus of Nola. Some Norman fonts are round; more often, perhaps, they are of square form, sometimes profusely decorated with grotesque imagery, and supported by a central massive circular stem. If we take away the sketchy chiselling, for which we have suggested a possible reason, no one would consider the St. Martin's font to be of Norman workmanship. Moreover, the sides of the font internally are extremely rough, and it is unlike the Normans to bestow so little in the way of finish.

We may conclude (as I have said) with some confidence that Ethelbert was baptised in St. Martin's Church. No traces have been discovered there of a baptistery—nor, indeed, of any in England before that erected (about 750) by Cuthbert, Archbishop of Canterbury, to the east of the Cathedral. But this does not militate against the theory that he was baptised by *affusion*, even though not from the present font notwithstanding traditional evidence to this effect in the seals before alluded to.

Reverence and probability alike protest against the idea, entertained by one or two distinguished antiquaries, that the font is nothing but the circular erection once surrounding the top of a well, or *puteus*, as depicted by Eadwin (1130-1174) in his plan of the herbarium of the cathedral.

Next to the font, we must direct attention to the "**West Wall of the Nave.**" Rugged and uneven as it now appears, there is still method in its building. Its general character is that of roughly-hewn Kentish rag-stones (with occasional blocks of chalk) bonded together by Roman bricks, arranged in sometimes a single, sometimes a double or even triple, course. Here and there a single course of stones lies between the courses of bricks, which are then 9 ins. apart. In other portions of the wall five or six courses of stone intervene between the courses of bricks, so that the courses of stones and bricks do not alternate regularly. The original face of the wall is much obscured by sundry patchings and repairs, and (on the north side) by the erection of a monumental tablet, lately removed to the tower-porch. In the centre, over the present

doorway, is an *arch* or opening, now filled up with courses of
Roman bricks and rubble of chalk or flint. The arch reaches
to a height of 17 or 18 ft. above the floor level, a few inches of
the crown having been cut away, and is on an average 7 ft.
2 in. wide. Whether it reached originally down to the ground,
or was merely an opening of the nature of a window, cannot be
positively settled, as the fillings-up have not yet been removed.

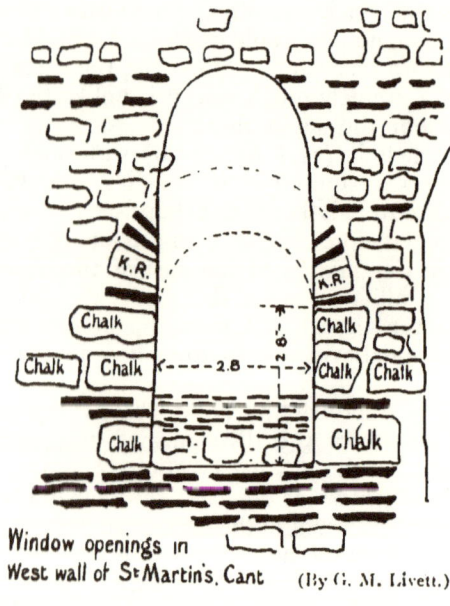

Window openings in West wall of St Martin's. Cant   (By G. M. Livett.)

On either side of the arch, at a distance of 2 ft., are two
windows (the upper 18 ins. of which, as they now appear, are
an extension made in Saxon or Norman times). The original
windows (below this extension) have their jambs of chalk-
blocks filled in with *white* mortar, while the arches are turned
in Roman bricks and rough voussoirs of Kentish rag-stone,
with interstices of bright *pink* mortar. These windows are
certainly built *more Romano*, and no sufficient evidence has
yet been brought forward to upset the opinion strongly held
by many archæologists—that they are *Roman*. The variation
of the mortar used in their construction from *white* mortar in

the jambs to *pink* mortar in the voussoirs of the arch is a very noticeable feature, and can be exactly paralleled in the Roman Pharos at Dover. It is certainly *prima facie*, a strong evidence of Roman workmanship. The windows are 2 ft. 8 in. wide, and would have measured 4 ft. from sill to crown. Their jambs are splayed at an angle that would allow about 12 ins. for the actual opening on the outer face of the wall. Their sills are respectively 9 ft. 9 in. and 10 ft. above the ground level, and the lower portion of the south window is filled up with thin mediæval tiles, such as we find here and there in the fourteenth-century tower, during the building of which the *extended* windows were undoubtedly blocked up. These *extended* windows have no voussoirs, but were cut out of the original walling, and simply plastered. Near them are portions of pink plaster still adhering to the wall.

Excavations have been made below the northern portion of this western wall in hopes of finding some of the original flooring of the church, but could not be further prosecuted because vaults, and even detached skeletons, were met with at a distance of only one foot below the existing pews.

The style of the north and south walls of the nave is much the same as that of the western wall; and behind the wood-work are considerable pieces of pink plaster, remarkable both for its hardness and texture. About this plaster we must say a few words, as it is, in our opinion, an important piece of evidence. It is composed of carbonate of lime imperfectly burned, of silicious sand, and pounded Roman brick, in almost equal proportions. It is true that some examples of this plaster have been occasionally found in Saxon, Norman, and even Early English buildings, but they are feeble imitations, distinguishable by the greater preponderance of sand, neither so bright nor crisp in section, more soft and pliable, and of a dullish colour. Two pieces of plaster were put side by side, one from St. Martin's and another from a Roman villa at Wingham, and to an experienced eye the texture was identical, except that the latter was rather thinner. And on our sending to such an undoubted expert as Mr J. T. Irvine (who had previously expressed much scepticism as to the Roman claims of St. Martin's, though he candidly confessed that he had not seen our recent explorations) a specimen of this plaster, he wrote in reply that, "both as regards texture of tile and lime mixture, and the colour produced thereby in section, it certainly seem to accord with that of *good Roman date.*"

About the middle of the north wall of the nave is a doorway, 4 ft. 2 in. wide, with jambs of Caen stones of irregular size, some of them showing marks of axe-tooling. The date of this doorway is uncertain. The head is destroyed and the rubble filling-up irregular, but the general appearance seems to favour the theory that it is Norman. On the east side of the doorway is a **stoup** for Holy Water, certainly of great antiquity. The shape is not regular, but it may be described roughly as measuring 20 by 17 inches.

At the south-east corner is the celebrated Norman **piscina**, said to be one of the earliest and most beautiful in England. The size of the actual opening is 13 by $7\frac{1}{2}$ inches with additional 4 inches to the top of the tympanum. Its jambs are of Caen stone, with the usual tool-marks. In it are three curious holes, two above and one below, penetrating about 2 inches into the stone. What these holes were intended for has been a great puzzle, but perhaps short poles were inserted in them which supported an ornamental canopy. It is not impossible that the piscina was originally placed somewhere nearer the east wall of the nave.

On the removal of the flooring beneath the piscina there was found a hole measuring 2 ft. by 1 ft. 8 in. and 5 ins. deep with a bottom of rough concrete, and 3 feet away were some **foundations of a wall** running parallel to the south wall. These foundations, chiefly consisting of flint, are about 18 ins. wide and 15 in. deep, though in parts rather fragmentary, and they were at first supposed to be connected with the parclose of the Altar of St. Nicholas, which formerly stood there. But Mr Livett opens out another possibility. He writes to us as follows:—"The portion of the east wall of the Nave, into which the south respond of the Chancel Arch is bonded, is similar in character and material to the brick walling of the western part of the *Chancel*, with which therefore, rather than with the *Nave*, it must be identified in date and construction. The same may be said of the corresponding bit of wall on the north side, which, however, has been more interfered with by the bondings of later work. In the face of the bit of wall on the south side, though rough and plastered with hard cement, may be detected the broken bonders of a wall that formerly ran westwards from it, and exactly in a line with the south wall of the Chancel. The vertical line of the junction of the southern face of the

NORMAN PISCINA.
(From a Photograph by Miss M. Bruce.)

destroyed wall with the bit of wall under examination can be traced clearly. It has all the proper signs of bonding, precisely similar in treatment to the signs of bonding seen on the face of the south wall of the Chancel immediately above the foundations of the Adjunct. The foundations discovered under the flooring of the Nave are in a position to have carried this destroyed wall. Though they are fragmentary, their material and depth correspond exactly with the foundations of the Chancel wall below the brick footings thereof. I drew Mr W. H. St. John Hope's attention to the signs of bonding which I have described, and from recent correspondence with him I infer that he accepts the evidence as sufficient to prove the former existence of a destroyed wall. The recovery of this wall running in the direction described, and contemporaneous in date with the western part of the Chancel, is an important factor in the consideration of the relative dates of the existing Chancel and Nave."

Before quitting the nave, the beautiful open roof of which deserves admiration, we must say a few words about a door or window opening from the west wall into the tower. This is of the Decorated period, and was perhaps connected with a tower-chamber (used in many old churches, both as a sleeping-room, and for a study); or the watchers, who guarded the church, would be able to see from thence the shrines with their relics and jewels, or it may have been to enable the sacristan to know the exact moment for ringing the Sanctus bell at the elevation of the Host, so that the sick in their chambers, the labourers in the fields, and the faithful in the church might join in a common act of adoration.

Let us now proceed to the **chancel**. The whole of the modern stalls were temporarily removed with a view of facilitating further investigations underground; but here, as in the nave, the excavations were almost entirely put a stop to by the existence of vaults and graves, extending right up to the walls on either side.

Owing to various circumstances, it has not been considered advisable, for the present, to strip the plaster from the chancel walls above the height of seven or eight feet, or east of the altar rails. Enough, however, has been done to show clearly that the present chancel may be assigned to two, and probably to three, distinct periods. For a distance of twenty feet eastward on each side of the chancel arch, the walls are built of Roman bricks laid evenly upon one another, *four bricks* (as I have before said), with their interstices of mortar, occupying *one foot*. This portion of the church shows very careful workmanship. It has been attributed by some to the time, and even the

Noakes, Canterbury, Photo.

CHANCEL OF ST. MARTIN'S (SHOWING SEDILE, SAXON DOORWAY, Etc).

personal supervision, of St. Augustine himself, but we think
that with greater probability it may be considered as *Roman*
building.

We have already described the square-headed doorway, but
may add that (during the present spring) the lepers' window
has been traced inwards to a depth of 1 ft. 8 in. from

SEDILE.
(From a Photograph by Miss M. Blore.)

the exterior of the wall. From this *square-headed* doorway
the *semi-circular* one (commented on in our description of
the exterior of the church) is 4 ft. 2 in. distant. Beyond
this the early brick wall extends eastward for 6 ft. 9 in.
till we reach a break in it, which was clearly the termination
of the original chancel. For the last two feet the work is
somewhat irregular, and from this circumstance, and from some
evidence discovered at this spot on the outside, it has been

conjectured that here we have the beginning of a Roman apse (cf. Appendix C). Eastward of this break, the walling is of different workmanship, showing with the mortar-joints six bricks to a foot, and after 3 ft. 5 in. we come to a **Sedile**, which was blocked up with mediæval brickwork, and opened out a short time ago. It had apparently a slightly pointed arch, of which about five inches have been cut away. The springing line is about 2 ft. 9½ in. above the seat; the radii are about 3 ft. 9 in., their centres being on the springing line. This would fix its measurements as follows:—Span, 5 ft.; depth, about 1 ft. 3 in.; height from seat to springing line, 2 ft. 9½ in.; and from seat to apex, about 6 ft. 4 in. A difficulty has arisen as to the date of the sedile from the fact that the top of it has been cut away by the insertion of a lancet window, appearing at first sight to belong to the Early English period, so that the sedile would seem as if it must be of an earlier date than the window. But Mr Livett, though believing it not impossible that the sedile and lancet window were built at the same time, and the sill of the window altered afterwards, thinks it more probable that the sedile and its adjoining brickwork were built late in the twelfth century, and the lancet window inserted subsequently, perhaps in the fourteenth century. The position of the sedile would seem to point out that the high altar stood, in Early English times, immediately east of the step whereon the present altar rails are placed.

The east wall of the church was partially pulled down and rebuilt about fifty years ago, to which period we owe the pseudo-Norman work of the reredos. The lancet windows were filled at that time with an ill-drawn representation of the Crucifixion in the centre, and on each side with the Ten Commandments, which were slowly fading away.

Inside the altar rails is an **aumbry**, 15 by 14 inches, with a wooden door of "linen pattern," dating probably from the time of Henry VII. The recess inside the door extends to a depth of 18 inches, and is still in use.

On the north side of the chancel is an arch surmounting a tomb, the oolite slab of which measures 6 ft. 6 in. long by 2 ft. wide at the top, and 1 ft. 6 in. wide at the foot. This tomb is apparently ancient. On the slab is an incision that probably contained a cross. At the back of the recess, in the wall, is an elegant Latin inscription, composed by Bishop Claughton (of St. Albans) and placed on a brass there by Canon Chesshyre, a former rector, to this effect: "If by chance anywhere near here lie the remains of Bertha, wife of

(SO-CALLED) QUEEN BERTHA'S TOMB.

King Ethelbert, let them rest in peace till the last coming of the Lord Jesus."

The arch above the tomb is a poor imitation of a Norman one, and stands under a curious round-headed opening in the wall, which may mark the position of a Norman window.

This tomb was always shown as "Queen Bertha's," and is still often called so even in the present day, owing to the statement that the queen was buried "in porticu Sancti Martini": but this, of course, refers to the apse or transept of St. Martin's Chapel in the monastery church of St. Augustine, where Bertha was laid on the south side of the altar.

The tomb was opened on January 12th, 1883, and beneath the covering slab of oolite was discovered a coffin of stone, hollowed out into the shape of the body, and having a small semi-circular opening (about 9 inches in diameter) for the head of the corpse. This latter opening had been bricked off from the rest of the tomb, and was thus formed into a receptacle for fragments of bones and other human remains, the rest of the coffin being filled up with flints, bricks, and rubbish. The bones were pronounced by a surgeon who was present to be probably those of an elderly man, aged about seventy years, and of small proportions. This was an apparent confirmation of a theory previously broached—viz. that the tomb possibly contained the remains of the restorer of the church in the thirteenth century. But alas for hasty conclusions! We have since ascertained that the tomb had been opened before 1844, and, so far as one can trust to oral tradition, it was then empty, except for a little human dust. Our informant also told us that there was a small cross, made of grass, which crumbled away when exposed to the air, but he was evidently confusing this with the cross made of two twigs that was found at the opening of Henry IV.'s tomb in the Cathedral.

Where, then, did the bones come from? There is an arch of an Edwardian monument in the vestry, but no coffin underneath; and our conjecture is that, when the present vestry (a kind of recess) was thrown out from the church, the tomb, which stood in the way, was moved back to its outer wall, and the bones were transferred to the so-called tomb of Queen Bertha. It is possible that the coffin-lid found in the square-headed Roman doorway was also taken from the same source.

So far as we can ascertain, no authentic records were kept at the time of the restoration of the church in 1844-45, which was done without a faculty. There is no doubt that its condition then was very dilapidated, and that we owe almost its actual preservation to the munificent liberality of Mr Daniel Finch and the careful judgment of its rector, Canon Chesshyre; but we must necessarily regret the absence of full particulars, and the opportunities that were then lost of exploring thoroughly the walls, floors, and general antiquities of the church.

On the top of the wall-plate was found a very interesting **chrismatory**, lately in the possession of Mrs Chesshyre of Barton Court, but now placed in a vestry-drawer used as a museum for curiosities connected with the church. It cannot lay claim to the same renown as the **ampulla** said to have been

CHRISMATORY (SHUT).
(From a Photograph by Mrs W. A. Lochée.)

used at the baptism of Clovis, when legend relates that the clerk who bore the chrism was prevented by the crowd from reaching his proper station, and, as the moment of unction arrived, St. Remi raised his eyes to heaven and prayed, "when lo ! suddenly a dove, white as snow, flew towards him, bearing down in his beak an ampulla filled with chrism from above."

Not even the most enthusiastic devotee of St. Martin's could claim this chrismatory as having been used at the baptism of Ethelbert, for it is clearly of the date of the fourteenth century.

At a meeting of the Society of Antiquaries on December 16th, 1880, it was thus described :—" It is a brass box 6 inches long, 2 inches broad, and 2 inches high. The lid is high-pitched, with slanting gable-ends nearly equilateral, and surmounted by a vertical crest or ridge pierced with quatrefoils. The extreme height of the lid is $2\frac{3}{8}$ inches ; that of the vertical crest is $\frac{7}{8}$ inch. The lid is attached behind by two hinges, each $\frac{1}{2}$ inch broad, and of which the raised plates are riveted to the back and lid of the box. The lid is fastened, not locked, by a hasp attached by a plate, and dropping on to a moveable catch on the face of the box. The upper and lower edges of the box, and its ridge, are mounted with mouldings attached by rivets. On opening the lid we found three oil-pots, all of them in fragments, and to none of them are the lids still remaining. At the bottom of the pots, however, are traces of some fibrous material. The pots, unlike the box itself, are of pewter." The necessity of keeping the three oils —(1) the holy chrism, (2) the oil for the sick, (3) the oil for catechumens—in distinct compartments is insisted upon by Archbishop Ælfric : "Ye ought to have three flasks ready for the three oils, for we dare not put them together in one oil vessel, because each of them is hallowed apart for a particular service."

The oil was contained in tow or cotton wool on a metal prong, and so moistened either the thumb of the priest or the person of the sick.

On the wall pierced through by the new vestry arch some remains were discovered of an old fresco, which represents the Crucifixion of our Lord, with St. John and the Blessed Virgin standing before the Cross. From the character of the painting (which was copied at the time), we are inclined to assign it to the fourteenth century.

At the same part of the church, while an opening was made ten years ago for the organ pipes, we came across some solid oak beams running horizontally. They are extremely hard, though worm-eaten on the surface : and resting as they were on the top of the wall (which consisted of eight feet of Roman brick and six feet of apparently rough Saxon work), at the height of fourteen feet from the ground, they may have formed portions of a Saxon roof.

The floor of the chancel is in part occupied by sepulchral slabs; one to Sir John Finch (whose monument is described below), which has the following inscription :—" Here is committed to the Earth, that it may return to Earth, whatever was mortal of John Finch, Baron Fordwich, of the ancient and noble family of Eastwell, whom it pleased, in preference

CHRISMATORY (OPEN) SHOWING THE THREE OIL-POTS.

to any epitaph, to have this inscribed on his sepulchral stone, ' Here lies the most humble servant of the best of Kings.' "

Another is that of Sir Henry Palmer of Howletts, father of thirteen children, obiit December 10th, 1659. A third of Maria, wife of Edward Keddell, of the Society of New Inn, London, obiit 1659, ætat: twenty. The descendants of this Keddell are now flourishing in America. The latter stone was removed when the new tile pavement was laid down, and placed in the immediately adjacent wall. It is described in a record of the last century as having been at that time in the *Nave.*

There are also two brasses, side by side, in a state of perfect preservation. The one to the south is in memory of Michael Fraunces, with a Latin inscription: "Here rest beneath this marble the bodies of Michael Fraunces, gentleman, and of Jane his wife, daughter of William Quilter, Esquire. The wife died on the 4th, the husband on the 10th, of January 1587. Their souls are in the enjoyment of heaven." The brass on the north side contains an effigy, and the following words written underneath: "Here lyeth Thomas Stoughton, late of Ashe, in the countie of Kent, gentleman, who *depted* this life the xiith of June 1591." Between and around these brasses is a tesselated pavement, not unlike a Roman pattern. A great part of it is modern, but some portion was pronounced by Mr Minton's chief workman to be very old, and it is not impossible that a few of the tiles may date from a pre-Norman period.

Fig. 1.   Fig. 2.

There is also, just at the entrance to the Sacrarium, a small cross let into the floor, which is apparently the one described by Hasted, who speaks of it as a "Cross of white marble, which has been much noticed by the curious as of great antiquity. It is about nine inches long and six wide." He gives a representation of it, which, however, is inaccurate, for he represents it as of this shape, as fig. 1, whereas in reality it is as fig. 2, and its dimensions are 18 inches by 6½ inches. We can only account for this variation by supposing that the upper part of the cross had been in his time sunk into the ground, and partially covered by the pavement.

The largest, and perhaps the principal, monument on the walls is a cumbrous one on the south of the Sacrarium, to John

Finch, Baron Fordwich, who is described as Advocate-General and Chancellor of Queen Henrietta Maria, Justice of the Court of Common Pleas, Privy Councillor, and Keeper of the Great Seal. He is remarkable in history as having been the Speaker of the House of Commons in the reign of Charles I., who was held down in his chair by Hobbes and others, in order that the protest against the infraction of the Petition of Right might be passed.

"Full of offices, full of days, he migrated hence to the Ancient of Days," aged 77, on November 20, 1660.

Beneath the monument there used to stand an altar-tomb enclosed with iron rails, and on a tablet near some Latin verses, composed by Charles Fotherby in the time of Charles II., "to a very noble and distinguished man."

The other monuments in the church are not of any general interest. Several of those mentioned by Hasted have already disappeared, including one to Giles Talbot, rector, in 1524.

The **Bells** are three in number. One of them has no inscription, the second bears simply the date 1641, and on the third, in old English characters, is the legend "Sancta Caterina, ora pro nobis."

Little need be said about the modern restorations and additions. The panelling of solid foreign oak, including the pews, was inserted by Mr Daniel Finch in 1844. A new pulpit and stone credence-table have also been added: the floor of the chancel has been re-tiled; the former vestry has been turned into an organ-chamber; and, where the organ once stood, a new vestry has been made. In it are placed old engravings of the church and a copy of the fresco which has already been described. In the drawer-museum there are kept, besides the chrismatory, some Saxon beads, fac-similes of the Merovingian coins, portions of the Roman (heathen) altar, and some pieces of pink plaster. The altar, altar cross, candle-sticks, etc., are new, as well as a large majority of the stained glass windows, in which the leading idea has been, as far as possible, to perpetuate events or persons connected with early Christian history. The three lights of the east window represent St. Augustine (1) landing at Ebb's Fleet, (2) entering Canterbury down St. Martin's Hill, and (3) baptising King Ethelbert; also (4) Queen Bertha attending Christian worship. In other windows of the chancel are pictures of the death of

St. Martin, and the closing scene in the life of the Venerable Bede ; while in the vestry are two single figures, erroneously supposed to be those of Pope Gregory and Bishop Lindhard, which were purchased some fifty years ago in Wardour Street.

On the south side of the **Nave** is a window representing various scenes in the Life of St. Martin—*e.g.* his entrance into the army, his consecration as bishop, his healing a leper, etc.— while in the baptistery is the well-known incident in the Forum at Rome, "Non Angli sed Angeli." In a memorial window on the north side, near the pulpit, are four female figures—Queen Bertha, her daughter St. Ethelburga, St. Dorothea, and St. Margaret of Antioch ; and in the north-west a picture of St. Martin dividing his cloak, probably copied from Vandyke. This latter window, as well as one in the tower, was painted in 1851 by a Miss Harriet Ludlow Clarke, who died at Cannes in 1866, and was a lady of some taste and distinction.

The **Churchyard**, practically the only one now in use in Canterbury, though St. Gregory's and St. Dunstan's church-yards are open for occasional interments, has come to be regarded as the "Campo Santo" of the city. In modern times the ground has been opened to receive the remains of many distinguished priests and laymen, among whom we may mention Dean Alford, Dean Payne-Smith, Bishop Parry and Canon Robertson (the ecclesiastical historian). Not very far from the lych-gate is a curious floriated cross, the legend on which seems to have puzzled many writers on the history of the church, though it bears distinctly on the front "Hew Whyte," and on the back "and Alys his wife." It is very probable that this is not a memorial cross, but a finial gable cross removed from the east of the chancel roof, and originally placed there in 1484 by Hew Whyte, who was a benefactor to the church. The cross has had many adventures. It was taken from the churchyard during the last century, and about thirty years ago was reposing as an ornament in the garden of a Canterbury citizen, but was brought back in 1876, and mounted on a pedestal.

In the *Valor Ecclesiasticus*, compiled in the twenty-sixth year of King Henry VIII., the value of the living for "tithes predyall and personal, oblations, and other spiritual yearly profits" is estimated at £9, and the yearly tenths at 18s., which, in the first year of Edward VI., were reduced to £6, 5s. and 12s. 2d.

respectively. Hasted remarks that in 1588 it was valued at
£20, and there were 71 communicants. In 1640 it was
valued at £40, with 70 communicants. And it appears by
the Survey of the King's Commissioners in the second year of
the reign of Edward VI. that there were *obit* lands given and
bequeathed by divers persons, that one yearly *obit* should be
kept in this church for ever : the yearly value of which lands
was 23s. 4d., of which the distribution to the poor was 12d.,
and outgoings 21d., leaving 20s. 7d. clear. Among the
charities bequeathed we find

(1) *Stephen Falkes* (1506) ordered that the yearly rents
and profits coming off the little messuage, with its appur-
tenances, in which Gregory Bradley then dwelt, should wholly
remain to the churchwardens of St. Martin's for ever, for the
reparation of the church.

(2) *Sir Henry Palmer*, Knt., of Bekesbourne (probably the
father of the Sir Henry Palmer now interred in the chancel),
by his will in 1611 gave 10s., to be yearly paid out of his
Manor of Well Court, to the minister and churchwardens of
the parish towards the relief of the poor of St. Martin's.

Both these charities have disappeared, but there are still in
existence (3) the bequest of *Dame Mabella Finch* of £100, to
be paid into the hands of Mr Bingham, and three such other
of the ablest inhabitants of the parish of St. Martin, to be by
them and the churchwardens and overseers of it, and their
successors for ever, employed for the use and benefit of the
then and hereafter poor of this parish. (An annuity of £10
bequeathed at the same time to the rector, and his successors,
has disappeared.)

(4) *James William Bain* left (in 1861) the sum of £100
Consols, the proceeds to be expended for the repair of his
tomb from time to time, and any residue for the benefit of the
poor of the parish.

The population of the parish at the last census was 211,
and the nett annual value of the benefice is estimated at £220.

The **Registers** date only from 1662, the preceding
Registers having been lost. No entries whatever are found in
them except the bare enumeration of births, marriages, and
deaths.

The church was originally exempt, and is still exempt (as
we have stated before), from the jurisdiction of the Archdeacon

of Canterbury. The patronage of the living continued solely
in the hands of the Archbishop of Canterbury till the church
was united, in 1681, with the neighbouring church of St. Paul,
by the mutual consent of the Archbishop and the Chapter of
Canterbury, the patrons of the latter. For nearly two hundred
years after this time the patronage was vested in the Archbishop, and Dean and chapter, alternately, until a few years
ago, when it was transferred back to the Archbishop alone.

Hasted gives a full account of the manor of Caldicot, lying
within the *Borough of St. Martin*, which was part of the
possessions of the see of Canterbury, and is thus described
in Domesday Book: "The archbishop himself holds the
Ville, which is called St. Martins: it belongs to Estursete,
and lies in that hundred ; it was taxed at one suling and one
half . . . In demesne there are two carucates and thirty-six
borderers. To this land there belong seven burgesses in
Canterbury, paying eight shillings and fourpence : there are
five mills of twenty shillings, and a small wood." Canon
Scott Robertson contended, in an able article on the "Saxon
Ville of St. Martin," that, as this is contained in the survey of
Aldington, the said ville was a limb of the manor of Aldington, and is therefore connected with the oratory of St. Martin
at Romney. But he was clearly mistaken—the ville is distinctly said to "pertain to Estursete, and to lie in that
hundred," which is now named Westgate, in Canterbury.
When Lanfranc divided the estates of the archbishop from
those of the newly-formed chapter, the different estates were
variously grouped together under the larger manors, and
sometimes shifted from one to another, for the convenience
(no doubt) of their management. The manor was appro-
priated afterwards to the use of the archbishop's table, till
Archbishop Reynolds gave it, at the earnest desire of the
monks, "to the Prior and Convent, inasmuch as it was a
convenient place for them to retire to, and recreate themselves,
when they were wearied out and tired, it being at no great
distance from their Monastery."

In the time of Edward I. a question arose whether the
Borough of St. Martin's was within the Liberties of the
city, and the jury found "that in future it should be subject
and answerable with the rest of the Citizens in all those
matters which belong to the Crown : that all residents and

dwellers in the borough ought to come four times a year to the hundred of Burgate, at the summons of the bailiffs of the city. And in like manner that they ought to come to the Portmote of the City, as often as the citizens should cause a common meeting to be summoned by the blowing of the horn."

"And so we leave *St. Martin's.* Only we wish that for the venerable antiquity of the Church and some time Episcopal estate of the place—things that have much dignified

ST. MARTIN'S.

(From an Old Print.)

both—it may always flourish in the maintenance of its due rights and respects." With these words of an old writer, we may conclude our description of the church. In an **Appendix** we have summed up a few remarks on the controversy that has been raging for the last few years as to the exact origin of the building. Those who argue against its Roman date bid us be content with the assurance that it is undoubtedly the oldest church in England, and tell us that, when St. Augustine knew it, it was small, but quite large enough for the small body of Christians who came over here with Queen Bertha, that it was probably built for her and them, though

it may have been on the site of a British church. This gives
us a continuous record of 1300 years and more. But we are
not content! for we believe that it is the oldest existing church
in *Europe*. Older than the churches of St. Maria Maggiore
and St. Pudenziana in Rome; than St. Croce, St. Francisco,
St. Vitale, St. Apollinare in Classe and St. Apollinare Nuovo
at Ravenna. Such churches as St. John Lateran, St. Paolo
fuori le Mura and St. Clemente cannot enter into the comparison, for they have been almost entirely rebuilt — and
in France and Germany nothing has survived down to our
own time, except a few fragments of the many large churches
constructed during the Roman occupation. We all desire that
truth should prevail; but that truth must be established by
intimate acquaintance with every detail of the building and a
knowledge of the latest explorations, and not depend on facts
accepted from hearsay, or a desire to establish any precon-
ceived theory.

Whatever be the decision ultimately arrived at, none can
doubt that *St. Martin's* is one of our grandest historical monuments. Small as it is, it may yet vie with the magnificent
cathedral of Christ Church in the glorious associations that have
clustered round its hallowed walls, and in point of antiquity
surpasses it by several centuries. It has witnessed the progress of the English nation from barbarism to civilisation.
The ever-widening stream that has continued to flow from
that tiny spring cannot fail to impress the earnest Christian
with a lesson of trust in the mysterious ways of Providence.
It has preserved its light burning almost continuously from
the time of the small band of British Christians, of the worship
of pious Queen Bertha and the great St. Augustine, down to
that solemn commemoration of 1897, when within its sacred
walls were gathered the representatives of the English Church
which has spread into all quarters of the civilised and un-
civilised world.

APPENDIX A

PROBABLE DATE OF INSTITUTION.

John de Charleton	1314
Robert de Henney . . .	1316
John de Bourn	1330
William de Castro . . .	1333
John de Byngham	1349
Richard de Camsale . .	1349
Robert Hayward	1381
Thomas Bolter . . .	1392
John Vag	1392
Robert Hubbyn . . .	1408
John Lovelych . . .	1419
Thomas Wotten . . .	1428
William Welton . . .	1434
Robert Hunt . . .	No date
John Bernard . . .	1448
John Skye	1456
John Browne . . .	1466
Giles Talbot . . .	1509
William Heynys . . .	1524
John Hichecocke . . .	1539
Thomas Nicholls . . .	1547
John Smyth . . .	1552
David Robson . . .	1560
Adam More . . .	1576
Eustace Ffrensham . . .	1578
John Mugge . . .	1578
John Stubbs . . .	1587
Richard Genvey . . .	1591
Matthew Warner . . .	1611
Rolando Vaughan . . .	1637
William Osborne . . .	1661
William Osborne (jun.) . .	1665
Owen Evans . . .	1681
Thomas Lamprey . . .	1743
John Airson . . .	1761
Thomas Freeman . . .	1788
Thomas Antony Mutlow . .	1808
J. E. N. Molesworth . .	1829
J. Stratton . . .	1839

LIST OF RECTORS.					PROBABLE DATE OF INSTITUTION.
W. J. Chesshyre	.	.	.	.	1842
Thomas Hirst	.	.	.	.	1859
A. B. Strettell	.	.	.	.	1874
Leslie E. Goodwin	.	.	.	.	1882
Leonard J. White-Thomson	.	.	.	.	1894

Thomas Bolter exchanged with **John Vag**, who was incumbent of the chantry in the hospital of St. Thomas at Eastbridge, in the city of Canterbury.

John Skye exchanged with **John Bernard.** He had formerly been rector of Dibdin, Hants.

John Browne, a chaplain, became rector on the resignation of John Skye.

William Heynys signed the Renunciation of the Papal Supremacy in 1534-5.

Eustace Ffrensham became insane.

APPENDIX B

DATE OF THE CHURCH

The revelation of fresh features of interest in the church by the recent explorations has attracted wide attention, and revived the controversy as to the probable date of the building. The whole subject was discussed in the spring of 1896 at a meeting of the Society of Antiquaries in London, after an able paper read by Mr W. H. St. John Hope. The question was also brought prominently forward at the Canterbury meeting of the Royal Archæological Institute in July 1896. What the newspapers called "The Battle of St. Martin's" raged with unabated vigour during the week, and, although many opinions were expressed with that *positiveness* which is said to mark the true antiquary (a positiveness not always founded on personal knowledge), yet by some well-known experts no pains were spared, and no special and professional attainments were wanting, to determine the issue on a scientific basis. It may be true to the experience of human nature, but yet it seems a feeble conclusion, if we confess that after all this apparently exhaustive debate, the controversy on the main point is as much alive as ever.

Premising that by "the Chancel" is meant the original chancel extending 20 feet eastward from the nave, we may state the following four as the only theories that now hold the field :—

(1) A Roman date for the chancel, and a later Roman date for the nave.
(2) A Roman date for the nave, and a later Roman date for the chancel.
(3) A Roman date for the chancel, and a Saxon date for the nave.
(4) An early Saxon date for the chancel, and a later Saxon date for the nave.

Many of the architectural details bearing on the subject are so minute, and so highly technical, that they are not suitable to the character of this Appendix. We propose, therefore, to confine ourselves chiefly to broad

general features, and to narrow the controversy, in the first place, to the
question whether there still exists in the church any *Roman* workmanship,
or whether even the most ancient part of it must be assigned to the *Saxon*
period. It is difficult to avoid recapitulation of many points alluded to in
the handbook, but we may summarise the principal arguments in favour of
the *Roman* date of portions of the church as follows: (1) **History.**—It is
distinctly mentioned by Bede that there was (in 597) a church dedicated to
St. Martin, built while the Romans still occupied Britain. Now this is
direct testimony, to which great weight must be assigned, when we consider
the character and authority of the writer. He was born in 673—*i.e.* only
seventy-six years after the mission of Augustine, and sixty-nine years after
his death, and wrote his "Ecclesiastical History" in the first part of the
eighth century, taking the greatest possible pains to make it worthy of his
subject. His information with regard to the history of Christianity in Kent
was derived from Albinus, Abbot of St. Augustine's, who was himself a
pupil of Theodore (Archbishop of Canterbury in 668) the great consolidator
of the English Church. We are told that Albinus referred to the records
in his keeping, and sent Nothelm, a priest of London, to search the Archives
at Rome, where were preserved many valuable letters of Gregory the Great
and subsequent Popes. Considering, then, the extreme carefulness of Bede,
and the sources from which he derived his materials, we cannot imagine
any evidence (short of first-hand) more trustworthy and valuable. That he
should have written as he did, making a positive statement that the Church
was built during the Roman occupancy of Britain, while all the time it
owed its foundation to Queen Bertha or Augustine, is perfectly incredible.
The theory as to its foundation by Queen Bertha has nothing whatever to
justify it ; and were the idea, that it was founded by Augustine, true, would
it not in Bede's time have been an easily ascertained fact, capable probably of documentary proof, especially among those who were inmates of
Augustine's own monastery, and would have claimed St. Martin's Church
as a precious inheritance—the legacy of their founder? No one impugns
the general accuracy of Bede's narrative, and the value of such historical
evidence cannot be too strongly insisted upon, for it is infinitely more
weighty than any *a priori* arguments or negative criticism.

Let us then assume that there was a Roman church in existence on St.
Martin's Hill when Augustine came to Canterbury. Is there any evidence
to strengthen this assumption in the present building? And, first, as regards
the Nave. We have already alluded to what we consider the valuable evidence
supplied by the style and texture of the *pink* plaster, also the variation of
the mortar in the construction of the west windows from *white* mortar in the
joints to *pink* mortar in the voussoirs of the arch, as well as the Roman-
like character of the windows themselves. The objection that " Roman
windows were never splayed" may be met (*a*) by the general statement
that the introduction of light by means of a splay is so natural that the
idea could not have escaped a Roman builder, especially in countries
where there was less light than in Italy. Isidore of Seville, a contemporary of Gregory the Great, living in the midst of Roman work, must
be describing what were the distinctive features of windows around him
when he says " Fenestræ sunt quibus pars exterior angusta, et interior
diffusa est " ; and (*b*) Mr Roach Smith, in his " *Collectanea Antiqua,*" gives
several illustrations of Roman splayed windows at Arles, Vienne, etc.,

and we are informed that there is one at South Shields, mentioned by Mr Robert Blair, F.S.A.

The character of the walls in the nave of St. Martin's seems to us to agree pretty closely with the technical description of Roman masonry in this country as "chiefly constructed of stone or flint, according to the part of the country in which one or the other material prevailed, embedded in mortar, and bonded at certain intervals throughout with regular courses or layers of large flat bricks or tiles, which, from the inequality of thickness and size, do not appear to have been shaped in any regular mould."

The *Nave* then has strong claims to Roman origin, without any reference to the *Chancel*. Mr Livett, however, claims that, whatever be the date of the nave, the brickwork of the original *Chancel* is certainly earlier, and contends that "the oldest portion of the existing building comprises (1) the side walls of the chancel, extending for 20 feet ; (2) the foundations of the destroyed Adjunct that once stood on the south side of the chancel ; (3) a portion of the east wall of the nave on either side of the chancel-arch, and (4) certain foundations under the floor of the nave, supposed to be a continuation of the chancel side-walls." It is possible that he is rather too sanguine in concluding that a general agreement has been reached on these points. But, assuming (for the sake of argument) that the chancel is the earlier, then, if we can establish a reasonable probability of a Roman date for the nave, *cadit quæstio*, so far as the "pro-Saxon" controversialists are concerned. On the other hand, even though it be proved that the *Nave* is post-Roman, yet still the *Chancel* may be Roman, since it is in their opinion of confessedly greater antiquity.

Is there anything in the *Chancel* to militate against its Roman origin? It is built in *opus lateritium*, bricks laid evenly upon one another, an ordinary style of Roman masonry ; for instances of which we may refer to remains found at the Roman villas at Wingham and Darenth, at the Stud-fall Roman castrum at Lympne, the blocked sluice-gate in the Silchester city wall, and countless other places. Allusion has been already made to Mr Micklethwaite's paper on "Saxon Church Building," in which, perhaps somewhat too confidently, he assigns to the Saxon periods the churches of Reculver, Brixworth, St. Pancras, etc. etc. It is a remarkable fact that the plan of St. Martin's Church (either with or without its reputed eastern apse) does not in many essential points agree with the plan of a single one of the churches therein described. And yet, if we accept the date of St. Martin's as post-Roman, it must have been built within less than a hundred years of most of them. He lays special stress on the apparent identity of character between the work at *St. Pancras* and in the *Chancel of St. Martin's*, saying that the "date of one must be very near to that of the other," and as he does not believe that St. Pancras can be Roman, therefore the same may be predicated of St. Martin's. But he makes many assumptions to prove this, taking imaginary sketches and theories for ascertained facts. Even so, the shape of the supposed apse is different in the two, and there is no north porch at St. Martin's as there is at St. Pancras, and if it can be established (as seems likely from recent discoveries) that there was an original chancel-arch at St. Martin's west of the side-chapel, the dissimilarity is even more apparent.

It is outside our purpose to discuss the date of St. Pancras, though many authorities maintain the possibility of its Roman origin. But, granting (for the moment) that St. Pancras' Church was built or restored by Augustine (and this is the latest date assigned to it), the identity in plan and character of the two churches is disputable. Of course, taking St. Martin's as it now exists, there is no similarity whatever, either in regard to the masonry of the nave, or the general outline. There is more similarity (with the exception of the points above mentioned) between St. Pancras and the assumed shape of St. Martin's chancel. But here, too, are points of difference. The walls of *St. Pancras* are only 1 *ft.* 10 *in.* in thickness; they are constructed almost entirely of broken bricks, roughly cut to a triangular shape and fitted together in the core, the interstices being filled up with small bits of brick. The walls of St. Martin's chancel are 2 *ft.* 2 *in.* thick, and contain a much larger proportion of whole bricks, about 12 inches wide, laid side by side in each course, the interval between them being filled up with mortar and small stones. We may mention also the difference in the treatment of the division between nave and chancel. In the churches of St. Pancras, Reculver, Brixworth, Peterborough, Lympne, and Rochester there was a triple chancel-arch. In St. Martin's the space is too narrow to admit of any such arrangement. If we carry back the original building of St. Pancras to Roman times (and we must remember that King Ethelbert is said by Bede to have allowed the Italian Missionaries to build and repair *churches* in all places) we do away with the difficulty as "to the temple of the heathen god being built after the fashion of a Christian church."

We may pass over, as unworthy of serious discussion, the argument that St. Martin's cannot be a Roman church, because no existing Roman churches have yet been discovered in this country! and that it is not Roman because its ground-plan does not tally with the ground-plan of the Roman Church at Silchester. In the first place, we do not know what the original ground-plan of St. Martin's was, and it has not yet been definitely settled whether it may not have possessed side-aisles. And secondly, to contend that it cannot be Roman because it is unlike the church at Silchester would be to limit the capabilities of Roman builders to one monotonous design, perpetually and exactly reproduced for a century or more, which would be contrary both to reason and experience.

There is, however, one objection remaining which must be faced, because it is put forward with all the professional knowledge of a skilful architect. The nave of the church is described as "being built of old stuff used anyway just as it came to hand, and tells of a time when there were ruins near, at which the builders were free to help themselves—a state of things unlikely in Roman Kent, but likely enough after the wars which accompanied the English occupation." This seems a forcible argument, but it is not altogether borne out by facts, neither is it a fair description. That a great part of St. Martin's Nave is patchy and rudely built no one can deny; but let us consider what periods of destructiveness and neglect it would have passed through, supposing it to have been built in Roman times. Durovernum (Canterbury) was abandoned by the Britons flying before the Jutish invasion, and was at first left unoccupied by the conquerors themselves. Its site lay for many a year uninhabited and desolate; its very name was forgotten, and the church would naturally have fallen into a state of partial ruin. Restored at the coming of Queen Bertha, probably ravaged by the Danes, repaired and enlarged to a great extent in the Early English period, gradually falling once more into decay, in what condition should we expect its walls to be ? Even within the last thirty years some interesting features have been destroyed, and the walls have been carelessly patched. When we consider all this, are we surprised if parts of it look like old stuff used anyway ? But (as we have stated) this is not a correct description of the lower portion of the walls, especially where they have been comparatively preserved behind the woodwork of the present pews. And even if the description "old stuff," etc., be applicable to portions of the nave walling, the same description would equally apply to the undoubted Roman work in the Pharos at Dover.

Is there not, too, such a thing as a period of decadence in any style? Just as there is good and bad Saxon work, good and bad Norman work, so must there have been good and bad Roman work. We are told in an account of the Roman excavations at Silchester that "examination showed that the rubble masonry of the whole western range (of the basilica) was of a *very poor character.*" "The stones (in a part of the Roman wall of London) form a mere skin, between the tile bonding courses, to the thick *irregular* rubble core." In the same wall, above the bonding course of three rows of tiles at the ancient ground-level, "the body of the wall is composed throughout its height of masses of ragstone, with now and then a fragment of chalk, bedded *very roughly* in mortar which has been pitched in, not run in, sometimes with so little care as to leave occasional empty spaces amongst the stones." It seems useless to multiply quotations for the purpose of establishing an obvious fact—viz. that granting a general *idea* and method pervading a building (as, we believe, there is clearly in St. Martin's nave), it is quite possible that at a time of decadence, and in the hands of inferior (perhaps British) workmen, this idea should be somewhat roughly carried out. This would be eminently the case if we attribute the erection of the nave towards the close of the fourth century—not so very long before the Roman evacuation of Britain.

Since writing the above, we have been informed by Mr Micklethwaite that he places the nave of St. Martin's as dating from the seventh century—but he gives no reason for doing so, except that he thinks the form of the western windows and some other things about the work indicate that period—and he acknowledges that there is nothing to fix the date closer. We have, however, at some length, pointed out reasons that seem to us to militate against his theory, and they need not be re-stated. Though his opinion is deservedly weighty, he has not been able to be present at any of the excavations.

APPENDIX C

Mr Livett has addressed to us the following communication with reference to the probability of there having been an eastern apse in the church,
and has furnished the subjoined sketches to illustrate his remarks :—

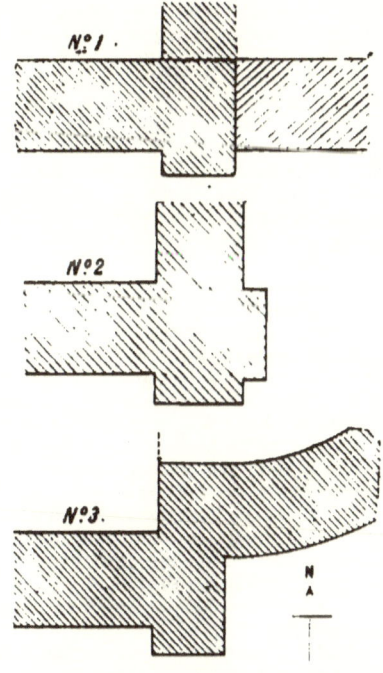

"No doubt exists in my mind that in the western half of the chancel
we have the oldest part of the existing church of St. Martin's, and I
am inclined to think that it is part of the first church built upon the site.
We must recognise, however, the possibility that the foundations of a
still earlier church remain undiscovered, either under the present nave or
elsewhere in the churchyard.

"The form of the *ground-plan* of the *early-brick* building (a term we have
agreed to use in reference to the masonry at the western half of the existing
chancel) has not been positively determined. Its eastern termination was

destroyed in the extension of the building in the late twelfth or early
thirteenth century, and its western end disappeared at a far earlier date.

" The probability that this early-brick building terminated eastward in
an apse is established by a careful consideration of the existing remains
of the south-east angle of that building, marked at the present time by
a narrow pilaster-buttress facing south, near the middle of the south wall
of the chancel. This buttress has been modernised, with its Caen-stone
quoins : but its foundations, lately exposed, prove that it accurately
represents, in dimension and position, an original early-brick buttress.
The sketches (given above) illustrate the features which indicate an apsidal
termination of the original building. *No.* 1 is a plan of part of the existing
south wall of the chancel. It shows the buttress, and, immediately east
of it, the junction of the twelfth-century wall with the early-brick wall.
To complete the description of existing features, it may be added that
the inner face of the wall (above some apparent foundations there underneath
the floor of the chancel) is rough—an evident sign that early-brick masonry
attached to this face was removed when the extension of the chancel was
made. Towards the east there are no signs to indicate where the destroyed
masonry stopped ; but towards the west there are, in the arrangement
of the bricks, marks of a vertical bonding-line, exactly corresponding in
position with the western face of the buttress on the outside. In that place,
then, the destroyed masonry originally rose with a clear face looking west.
How far that masonry ran towards the north there is nothing to show.
It is a significant fact—proved by the hole lately made through the twelfth-
century wall, at its junction with the earlier work—that the end of
the early-brick wall is in plane with the eastern face of the external buttress,
and that no buttress ever existed on the eastern face of the angle.

" All these features are consistent with the supposition that the early-brick
building terminated eastwards in an apse, and consistent with that supposition only. Had the east end been square, the natural treatment would
have been as shown in *Sketch No.* 2—there would remain indications of a
buttress on the eastern side of the angle, the vertical bonding-joint would
be seen farther west, to allow for an end wall of the same thickness
(2 ft. 2 in.) as the side-wall—and the existing buttress, instead of being
narrow, would probably be of the same breadth as the walls.

" *Sketch No.* 3 shows the natural treatment of an apsidal termination. It
explains the absence of a buttress on the eastern face of the angle, such
buttress being unnecessary in the case of an apse : and it explains the use
of the existing narrow buttress on the southern face, as serving to counter-
act the thrust of the facing-arch of the apse. No argument can be
drawn from the patch of foundations found under the floor near the wall—
and they do not at present run across the chancel ; but probably they did
so run originally, whether the end were square or apsidal, and have been
removed in the centre, to make room for burials.

" The position and arrangement of the west end of the early-brick building
cannot at present be determined. That there was a cross-wall along the
line of the present chancel-arch is certain. This is sufficiently proved by
unmistakable signs of a vertical bonding-joint on the face of the north
wall of the chancel, 2½ inches from the east face of the northern joint of
the chancel-arch. This joint allows for a cross-wall of exactly the normal
thickness of the early-brick walling. Moreover, you tell me that you have

seen bricks in such a position under the floor in this corner as to suggest a cross-wall. All signs of the corresponding vertical bonding-joint on the opposite side of the chancel have been removed in the patching of alterations which need not here be discussed. . . . I omitted to say that the evidence of the cross-wall is further strengthened by the remains of an external buttress embedded in the east wall of the nave on the south side. Similar evidence on the north side has been destroyed by the insertion of the small doorway leading from the nave into the modern vestry.

"With regard to the original arrangement of this part of the early-brick building, I am unable to make any conjecture that would satisfactorily explain all these features. The cross-wall may possibly have been the west wall of a small church: in which case the signs of building to the west of it must be connected with a porch or *atrium*. I think it more likely, however, that the cross-wall was the original division between the chancel and a destroyed nave, and contained a single chancel-arch. The original line of division between chancel and nave has, in most cases, though not invariably, been preserved throughout all enlargements of our churches. It may simply be said that there was a cross-wall as described: the evidence for it is final.

"The *adjunct*, the foundations of which were recently exposed, on the south side is important in this consideration: but I have not referred to it, partly because it has been fully dealt with elsewhere, and partly because (as I have said) I have no satisfactory suggestion for the entire restoration of the ground-plan; nor do I venture to suggest dates either for the early-brick building or for the nave. I am convinced that the nave is of later date than the early-brick work" (of the chancel).

W. H. WHITE AND CO. LTD.
RIVERSIDE PRESS, EDINBURGH

Bell's Cathedral Series.

EDITED BY

GLEESON WHITE AND E. F. STRANGE.

In specially designed cloth cover, crown 8vo, 1s. 6d. each.

Now Ready.

CANTERBURY. By HARTLEY WITHERS. 2nd Edition, revised. 36 Illustrations.

SALISBURY. By GLEESON WHITE. 2nd Edition, revised. 50 Illustrations.

CHESTER. By CHARLES HIATT. 24 Illustrations.

ROCHESTER. By G. H. PALMER, B.A. 38 Illustrations.

OXFORD. By Rev. PERCY DEARMER, M.A. 34 Illustrations.

EXETER. By PERCY ADDLESHAW, B.A. 35 Illustrations.

WINCHESTER. By P. W. SERGEANT. 50 Illustrations.

LICHFIELD. By A. B. CLIFTON. 42 Illustrations.

NORWICH. By C. H. B. QUENNELL. 38 Illustrations.

PETERBOROUGH. By Rev. W. D. SWEETING. 51 Illustrations.

HEREFORD. By A. HUGH FISHER. 40 Illustrations.

In the Press.

LINCOLN. By A. B. KENDRICK, B.A.	YORK. By A. CLUTTON BROCK, B.A.
DURHAM. By J. E. BYGATE.	WELLS. By Rev. P. DEARMER, M.A.
GLOUCESTER. By H. L. MASSÉ.	SOUTHWELL. By Rev. A. DIMOCK.

Preparing.

ST DAVID'S. By PHILIP ROBSON.	CHICHESTER. By H. CORLETTE,
ELY. By T. D. ATKINSON.	A.R.I.B.A.
WORCESTER. By E. F. STRANGE.	

ST ALBANS.	RIPON.	ST PAUL'S.
CARLISLE.		BRISTOL.

Uniform with above Series.

ST. MARTIN'S, CANTERBURY. By the Rev. CANON ROUTLEDGE. [*Ready.*

BEVERLEY MINSTER. By CHARLES HIATT. [*Preparing.*

Opinions of the Press.

"For the purpose at which they aim they are admirably done, and there are few visitants to any of our noble shrines who will not enjoy their visit the better for being furnished with one of these delightful books, which can be slipped into the pocket and carried with ease, and is yet distinct and legible. . . . A volume such as that on Canterbury is exactly what we want, and on our next visit we hope to have it with us. It is thoroughly helpful, and the views of the fair city and its noble cathedral are beautiful. Both volumes, moreover, will serve more than a temporary purpose, and are trustworthy as well as delightful."—*Notes and Queries.*

"We have so frequently in these columns urged the want of cheap, well-illustrated, and well-written handbooks to our cathedrals, to take the place of the out-of-date publications of local booksellers, that we are glad to hear that they have been taken in hand by Messrs George Bell & Sons."—*St James's Gazette.*

"Visitors to the cathedral cities of England must often have felt the need of some work dealing with the history and antiquities of the city itself, and the architecture and associations of the cathedral, more portable than the elaborate monographs which have been devoted to some of them, more scholarly and satisfying than the average local guide-book, and more copious than the section devoted to them in the general guide-book of the county or district. Such a legitimate need of 'Cathedral Series' now being issued by Messrs George Bell & Sons, under the editorship of Mr

Gleeson White and Mr E. F. Strange, seems well calculated to supply. The volumes are handy in size, moderate in price, well illustrated, and written in a scholarly spirit. The history of cathedral and city is intelligently set forth and accompanied by a descriptive survey of the building in all its detail. The illustrations are copious and well selected, and the series bids fair to become an indispensable companion to the cathedral tourist in England."—*Times*.

"They are nicely produced in good type, on good paper, and contain numerous illustrations, are well written, and very cheap. We should imagine architects and students of architecture will be sure to buy the series as they appear, for they contain in brief much valuable information." —*British Architect*.

"Half the charm of this little book on Canterbury springs from the writer's recognition of the historical association of so majestic a building with the fortunes, destinies, and habits of the English people. . . . One admirable feature of the book is its artistic illustrations. They are both lavish and satisfactory—even when regarded with critical eyes."— *Speaker*.

"There is likely to be a large demand for these attractive handbooks." —*Globe*.

"Bell's ' Cathedral Series,' so admirably edited, is more than a description of the various English cathedrals. It will be a valuable historical record, and a work of much service also to the architect. The illustrations are well selected, and in many cases not mere bald architectural drawings but reproductions of exquisite stone fancies, touched in their treatment by fancy and guided by art."—*Star*.

"Each of them contains exactly that amount of information which the intelligent visitor, who is not a specialist, will wish to have. The disposition of the various parts is judiciously proportioned, and the style is very readable. The illustrations supply a further important feature ; they are both numerous and good. A series which cannot fail to be welcomed by all who are interested in the ecclesiastical buildings of England."— *Glasgow Herald*.

"Those who, either for purposes of professional study or for a cultured recreation, find it expedient to ' do ' the English cathedrals will welcome the beginning of Bell's ' Cathedral Series.' This set of books is an attempt to consult, more closely, and in greater detail than the usual guide-books do, the needs of visitors to the cathedral towns. The series cannot but prove markedly successful. In each book a business-like description is given of the fabric of the church to which the volume relates, and an interesting history of the relative diocese. The books are plentifully illustrated, and are thus made attractive as well as instructive. They cannot but prove welcome to all classes of readers interested either in English Church history or in ecclesiastical architecture."—*Scotsman*.

"A set of little books which may be described as very useful, very pretty, and very cheap . . . . and alike in the letterpress, the illustrations, and the remarkably choice binding, they are ideal guides."— *Liverpool Daily Post*.

"They have nothing in common with the almost invariably wretched local guides save portability, and their only competitors in the quality and quantity of their contents are very expensive and mostly rare works, each of a size that suggests a packing-case rather than a coat-pocket. The ' Cathedral Series ' are important compilations concerning history, architecture, and biography, and quite popular enough for such as take any sincere interest in their subjects."—*Sketch*.

LONDON : GEORGE BELL AND SONS.

www.ingramcontent.com/pod-product-compliance
Lightning Source LLC
Chambersburg PA
CBHW032144010726
47493CB00008BA/2577